2004

The Old Farmer's Almanac

ENGAGEMENT

CALENDAR

—Beth Krommes

Useful Advice and Folk Wisdom from the Publisher of
The Old Farmer's Almanac

Copyright 2003 by Yankee Publishing Incorporated

Editorial staff: Janice Stillman, Mare-Anne Jarvela, Heidi Stonehill, Ellen Bingham,
Joyce Monaco, Martie Majoros

Cover and interior design by Margo Letourneau

Daily text information by Martha White
"Secrets of the Zodiac" by Celeste Longacre

Moon phases and other astronomical events are calculated in Eastern Standard Time,
or Eastern Daylight Time where applicable.

Cover art: *"Bouquet de Pensées," by Pierre Joseph Redouté. Choix des Plus Belles Fleurs.
Paris, l'auteur, C.L.F. Panckoucke [et al.], 1829.*
–courtesy Hunt Institute for Botanical Documentation, Carnegie Mellon University, Pittsburgh, Pa.

To order The Old Farmer's Almanac Engagement Calendar, call 800-223-3166,
or visit our Web site at **www.almanac.com**.

Printed in U.S.A.

ISBN 1-57198-291-4

2004

JANUARY
S	M	T	W	T	F	S
				1	2	3
4	5	6	7	8	9	10
11	12	13	14	15	16	17
18	19	20	21	22	23	24
25	26	27	28	29	30	31

FEBRUARY
S	M	T	W	T	F	S
1	2	3	4	5	6	7
8	9	10	11	12	13	14
15	16	17	18	19	20	21
22	23	24	25	26	27	28
29						

MARCH
S	M	T	W	T	F	S
	1	2	3	4	5	6
7	8	9	10	11	12	13
14	15	16	17	18	19	20
21	22	23	24	25	26	27
28	29	30	31			

APRIL
S	M	T	W	T	F	S
				1	2	3
4	5	6	7	8	9	10
11	12	13	14	15	16	17
18	19	20	21	22	23	24
25	26	27	28	29	30	

MAY
S	M	T	W	T	F	S
						1
2	3	4	5	6	7	8
9	10	11	12	13	14	15
16	17	18	19	20	21	22
23	24	25	26	27	28	29
30	31					

JUNE
S	M	T	W	T	F	S
		1	2	3	4	5
6	7	8	9	10	11	12
13	14	15	16	17	18	19
20	21	22	23	24	25	26
27	28	29	30			

JULY
S	M	T	W	T	F	S
				1	2	3
4	5	6	7	8	9	10
11	12	13	14	15	16	17
18	19	20	21	22	23	24
25	26	27	28	29	30	31

AUGUST
S	M	T	W	T	F	S
1	2	3	4	5	6	7
8	9	10	11	12	13	14
15	16	17	18	19	20	21
22	23	24	25	26	27	28
29	30	31				

SEPTEMBER
S	M	T	W	T	F	S
			1	2	3	4
5	6	7	8	9	10	11
12	13	14	15	16	17	18
19	20	21	22	23	24	25
26	27	28	29	30		

OCTOBER
S	M	T	W	T	F	S
					1	2
3	4	5	6	7	8	9
10	11	12	13	14	15	16
17	18	19	20	21	22	23
24	25	26	27	28	29	30
31						

NOVEMBER
S	M	T	W	T	F	S
	1	2	3	4	5	6
7	8	9	10	11	12	13
14	15	16	17	18	19	20
21	22	23	24	25	26	27
28	29	30				

DECEMBER
S	M	T	W	T	F	S
			1	2	3	4
5	6	7	8	9	10	11
12	13	14	15	16	17	18
19	20	21	22	23	24	25
26	27	28	29	30	31	

JANUARY

with *The Old Farmer's Almanac*

125 Years Ago

The morning salutation now is, A happy new year! But the great problem is to make it so, and that does not turn on outward circumstances so much as some suppose. The rich are not, as a class, happier than the poor. Mental activity is the source of contentment, and the busy brain makes the happy mind. The wisest of all petitions is, "Give me neither poverty nor riches." When Webster was asked what he thought was the best way to get through a spell of hot weather, his reply was "Keep busy, keep the mind at work, and you won't think of it." Life hangs heavy, and drags, on those who have nothing to do. There is always work on the farm; and these long winter evenings and crisp days can be filled so full that they will seem all too short, and we wonder where they have gone. Keep a sharp eye on the stock. Cows well wintered are half summered. Study their comfort. Give them good bedding, a few roots at fixed hours, and a daily carding. The barn cellar needs looking after. Mix the muck and the loam. Settle up old scores. It is a good plan to pay as you go; but if this can't be done, keep the accounts straight at least and get no deeper into the mud.

—The Old Farmer's Almanac

FULL-MOON LORE

The Full Wolf Moon occurs on January 7 in 2004. It is also known as the Old Moon. To some Native American tribes, it was the Snow Moon, but most applied this latter name to the February full Moon.

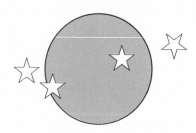

If there is no snow in January, there will be more in March and April.

JANUARY • 2004   FEBRUARY • 2004

S M T W T F S   S M T W T F S
        1 2 3   1 2 3 4 5 6 7
4 5 6 7 8 9 10   8 9 10 11 12 13 14
11 12 13 14 15 16 17   15 16 17 18 19 20 21
18 19 20 21 22 23 24   22 23 24 25 26 27 28
25 26 27 28 29 30 31   29

Make a point of buying a good hat.
–Ladies Indispensable Assistant, 1852

Friday

9

But all sorts of things and weather Must be taken in together To make up a year And a Sphere.
–Ralph Waldo Emerson, American writer (1803–1882)

Saturday

10

Massage varicose veins with witch-hazel water.

Sunday

11

REMINDERS

January

12 Monday

A pinch of baking soda in the cooking water keeps beans, spinach, and asparagus greener.

13 Tuesday

He who runs after wit is apt to embrace folly.
—The [Old] Farmer's Almanac, 1801

14 Wednesday

Last Quarter Moon

Find spring in seed catalogs; send your orders now.

15 Thursday

To store leftover egg yolks for a day or two, place them into a container, cover yolks with water, cap container, and refrigerate.

JANUARY • 2004 FEBRUARY • 2004

S	M	T	W	T	F	S
				1	2	3
4	5	6	7	8	9	10
11	12	13	14	15	16	17
18	19	20	21	22	23	24
25	26	27	28	29	30	31

S	M	T	W	T	F	S
1	2	3	4	5	6	7
8	9	10	11	12	13	14
15	16	17	18	19	20	21
22	23	24	25	26	27	28
29						

Friday **16**

It's a good time for interior painting. Always prime the knots in new wood.

Saturday **17**

Benjamin Franklin's Birthday

Idleness and pride tax with a heavier hand than kings and parliaments.
–Benjamin Franklin,
American statesman
(1706–1790)

Sunday **18**

To ward off colds, drink a blender shake of mangoes, kiwis, cantaloupe, and strawberries.

REMINDERS

JANUARY

19 *Monday*

*Our scientific power
has outrun our
spiritual power. We
have guided missiles
and misguided men.*
—Martin Luther King Jr.,
American civil rights leader
(1929–1968)

20 *Tuesday*

A group of fish
is a school;
toads, a knot;
chicks, a clutch.

21 *Wednesday*

New Moon

For greater success,
begin new ventures
with the new Moon.

22 *Thursday*

High seas come to the sailor
who dreams of horses.

JANUARY • 2004   FEBRUARY • 2004

S	M	T	W	T	F	S
				1	2	3
4	5	6	7	8	9	10
11	12	13	14	15	16	17
18	19	20	21	22	23	24
25	26	27	28	29	30	31

S	M	T	W	T	F	S
1	2	3	4	5	6	7
8	9	10	11	12	13	14
15	16	17	18	19	20	21
22	23	24	25	26	27	28
29						

Friday 23

Add a quart of
milk to your bath to
rejuvenate your
winter-dry skin.

Saturday 24

Motto for Aquarian's
dynamic Water Bearer
(Jan. 20 to Feb. 19):
"I universalize."

Sunday 25

If the temperature
is below freezing and
the barometer falls
two or three tenths
of an inch, expect
a thaw.

REMINDERS

January ❦ February

26 *Monday*

To enhance your immune system, make laughter a habit.

27 *Tuesday*

It is not enough if you are busy. The question is, what are you busy about?
–Henry David Thoreau, American writer (1817–1862)

28 *Wednesday*

Pesto sauce will keep its bright color in pasta that is cooked with a few drops of lemon juice.

29 *Thursday*

First Quarter Moon

Envy accomplishes nothing.
–Greek proverb

JANUARY • 2004

S	M	T	W	T	F	S
				1	2	3
4	5	6	7	8	9	10
11	12	13	14	15	16	17
18	19	20	21	22	23	24
25	26	27	28	29	30	31

FEBRUARY • 2004

S	M	T	W	T	F	S
1	2	3	4	5	6	7
8	9	10	11	12	13	14
15	16	17	18	19	20	21
22	23	24	25	26	27	28
29						

Friday **30**

New Year's resolutions slipping? Schedule time for them on your calendar.

Saturday **31**

Married when the year is new, he'll be loving, kind, and true.

Sunday **1**

Don't light a candle from the fireplace if you hope to grow rich.

REMINDERS

FEBRUARY

with The Old Farmer's Almanac

125 Years Ago

FARMER'S CALENDAR, FEBRUARY 1879

*D*ay by day brings with it the round of chores that do so much to sweeten life on the farm. Many a mouth waits for our coming, and the sound of the footstep is welcome. But we must keep up with the world and the best way to do it is to take some time to read and study. Now is the time, if ever. Get books that excite thought. To read for mere diversion of the mind is not enough. Little mental growth can come of that. We ought to cherish a sort of reverence for good books; they give us the richest of all legacies, the spiritual life of past ages, the society, the very thoughts of the greatest minds that ever lived. It is a sad mistake of any man, no matter what his work in life may be, to fail to cherish and cultivate a love for books. He loses by far the greatest charm which the world can ever give, and no amount of small talk can make up for it. We can often get a simple hint from a book that will put many a dollar in the pocket, but the chief end is mental growth. A mild day, now and then, will give us a chance to clean and air the cellar, to paint and fix up the tools, to cut and moisten the coarser food for cattle, and to look after the woodpile. Do not neglect the farmer's club. We must do our part for society as well as for ourselves.

—The Old Farmer's Almanac

FULL-MOON LORE

The Full Snow Moon occurs on February 6 in 2004. Usually, the heaviest snows of the year fall during this month. Hunting at this time of year became difficult for many Native American tribes, so they also called this the Hunger Moon.

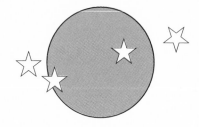

It takes three cloudy days to bring a heavy snow.

Secrets of the Zodiac

AQUARIUS

JANUARY 20–FEBRUARY 19

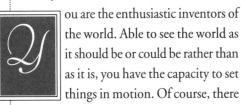

You are the enthusiastic inventors of the world. Able to see the world as it should be or could be rather than as it is, you have the capacity to set things in motion. Of course, there are a few of you out there who are more conservative, and if this is you, go back to January and read the Capricorn section.

Detached and impersonally friendly to all, you have many acquaintances. You are a dedicated humanitarian and very tolerant—of everything but intolerance. You function well in groups and organizations as long as you can maintain your independence. Freedom is extremely important to you, and you need to be able to do your work your own way.

You are often politically involved because you see certain ordinary aspects of our culture and society as truly strange. Needing to be different, some aspect of your personality will be seen as eccentric by others.

A MEAN, CLEAN COMPUTER SCREEN

■ Have smudges and built-up dust on your computer monitor made it difficult to read your e-mails? Gently wipe the screen with a clean cotton cloth slightly dampened with rubbing alcohol or a household window cleaner. If you prefer, you can make your own cleaning solution by mixing 1 part white vinegar with 10 parts water.

A FEW RULES TO KEEP IN MIND

- Always unplug the monitor before cleaning to avoid electrical shock.
- Never use an abrasive cleaner.
- Do not spray the cleaning solution directly onto the computer screen.

ORIGIN OF MONTH NAMES

PART II

July ■ Named to honor Roman dictator Julius Caesar (100–44 B.C.). In 46 B.C., Julius Caesar, with the help of Sosigenes, developed the Julian calendar, the precursor to the Gregorian calendar we use today.

August ■ Named to honor the first Roman emperor (and grandnephew of Julius Caesar), Augustus Caesar (63 B.C.–A.D. 14).

September ■ From the Latin word *septem*, "seven," because this had been the seventh month of the early Roman calendar.

October ■ From the Latin word *octo*, "eight," because this had been the eighth month of the early Roman calendar.

November ■ From the Latin word *novem*, "nine," because this had been the ninth month of the early Roman calendar.

December ■ From the Latin word *decem*, "ten," because this had been the tenth month of the early Roman calendar.

FEBRUARY

2 Monday

Groundhog Day
Candlemas

A bright, clear Candlemas means a late spring.

3 Tuesday

For insomnia, eat tomatoes, tangerines, or oranges.

4 Wednesday

Learn to read slow: all other graces Will follow in their proper places.
–William Walker, English educator (1623–1684)

5 Thursday

No dustpan? Substitute with a newspaper, wetting one edge to stick to the floor.

FEBRUARY • 2004   MARCH • 2004

S M T W T F S   S M T W T F S
1 2 3 4 5 6 7   1 2 3 4 5 6
8 9 10 11 12 13 14   7 8 9 10 11 12 13
15 16 17 18 19 20 21   14 15 16 17 18 19 20
22 23 24 25 26 27 28   21 22 23 24 25 26 27
29   28 29 30 31

Full Snow Moon

Friday

6

To mince garlic
or onions more easily,
sprinkle them
with salt.

Walk the dog to
reduce your stress and
burn off calories.

Saturday

7

To remove animal fur
from upholstery, rub
gently in a circular
motion with a slightly
damp sponge.

Sunday

8

REMINDERS

FEBRUARY

9   *Monday*

In order to seek one's own direction, . . . simplify the mechanics of ordinary, everyday life.
–Plato, Greek philosopher (427–347 B.C.)

10   *Tuesday*

Old habits are iron shirts.
–Yugoslav proverb

11   *Wednesday*

Eat more tomatoes (full of antioxidants) to reduce cancer risk.

12   *Thursday*

Abraham Lincoln's Birthday

Plant a 'President Lincoln' lilac—a pale-blue, single-blooming early variety.

FEBRUARY • 2004

S M T W T F S
1 2 3 4 5 6 7
8 9 10 11 12 13 14
15 16 17 18 19 20 21
22 23 24 25 26 27 28
29

MARCH • 2004

S M T W T F S
1 2 3 4 5 6
7 8 9 10 11 12 13
14 15 16 17 18 19 20
21 22 23 24 25 26 27
28 29 30 31

Last Quarter Moon

Friday

13

Pin bay leaves to your pillow
to dream of your beloved.

St. Valentine's Day

Saturday

14

For a love letter,
good paper is
indispensable,
. . . gold-edged,
perfumed, or
ornamented.
—*Ladies Indispensable*
Assistant, 1852

Susan B. Anthony's Birthday
(Fla.; Wis.)

Sunday

15

Men their rights
and nothing more;
women their rights
and nothing less.
—Susan B. Anthony, American
reformer (1820–1906)

REMINDERS

FEBRUARY

16 Monday

George Washington's Birthday
(observed)
Family Day (Alta., Can.)

*Allow children to be
happy in their own
way, for what better
way will they ever find?*
–Dr. Samuel Johnson, English
writer (1709–1784)

17 Tuesday

Moisturize chapped
lips with honey, leave
on overnight.

18 Wednesday

Popeye was wrong!
Spinach can hinder
iron absorption.

19 Thursday

On Thursday at three,
Look out, and you'll see
What Friday will be.
–English proverb

FEBRUARY • 2004

S M T W T F S
1 2 3 4 5 6 7
8 9 10 11 12 13 14
15 16 17 18 19 20 21
22 23 24 25 26 27 28
29

MARCH • 2004

S M T W T F S
1 2 3 4 5 6
7 8 9 10 11 12 13
14 15 16 17 18 19 20
21 22 23 24 25 26 27
28 29 30 31

New Moon

Friday 20

The new and first quarter Moon phases are best for grafting trees.

Saturday 21

Emotions run deep with Pisces the Fish (Feb. 20 to Mar. 20), whose motto is "I believe."

Islamic New Year

Sunday 22

Who is wise? He that learns from everyone.
–Benjamin Franklin, American statesman (1706–1790)

REMINDERS

FEBRUARY

23 *Monday*

Married in February's
sleepy weather,
Life you'll tread in time
together.

24 *Tuesday*

Mardi Gras (Ala.; La.)
Shrove Tuesday

Pancakes are
traditional today.

25 *Wednesday*

Ash Wednesday

A full belly makes a
dull brain.

26 *Thursday*

. . . such a February face,
So full of frost, of
storm, of cloudiness.
—William Shakespeare,
English playwright
(1564–1616)

FEBRUARY • 2004   MARCH • 2004

S	M	T	W	T	F	S
1	2	3	4	5	6	7
8	9	10	11	12	13	14
15	16	17	18	19	20	21
22	23	24	25	26	27	28
29						

S	M	T	W	T	F	S
	1	2	3	4	5	6
7	8	9	10	11	12	13
14	15	16	17	18	19	20
21	22	23	24	25	26	27
28	29	30	31			

Heritage Day (Y.T., Can.)
First Quarter Moon

Friday 27

Repot houseplants
now for a breath
of spring.

Sleep at least
seven hours; it boosts
your immunity and
mental acuity.

Saturday 28

Sunday of Orthodoxy

Sunday 29

Begin new projects on
Leap Day (today).

REMINDERS

MARCH

with *The Old Farmer's Almanac*

125 Years Ago

The bluebird and the robin, welcome guests, come to cheer us with their modest song, and the brooks that were bound in ice run leaping and sparkling with new life. Every living thing seems to be glad. No want of work now. There are the tools to fix up, the wood to be chopped, the harness to clean, the fences to mend, and the stock to be fed. The cows are to come in soon, and need more care. Feed lightly two or three weeks before the time comes, and give them a warm pen where there are no cold drafts. The best cows are most apt to have trouble with the bag at this feverish time, and some farmers wash it in cold water, and keep the calf on to bunt it down as they say. This is all wrong. If the bag is swollen, sore, and inflamed, bathe it every two hours in hot soap-suds, rubbing it long and gently, and drying it with woollen rags each time. Never touch cold water to a caked udder; you run the risk of loss of the glands. Hot soap-suds well followed up, and patient rubbing, will soon bring it all right. Feed no meal or feverish food for a week or so. Just after calving, a pail of warm water, with a pint of rye meal stirred in, may be given three or four times a day.

—The Old Farmer's Almanac

FULL-MOON LORE

The Full Worm Moon occurs on March 6 in 2004. The ground begins to soften and earthworm casts reappear, inviting the return of robins. This Moon is also known as the Sap Moon, because it marks the time when maple sap begins to flow and the annual tapping of maple trees begins.

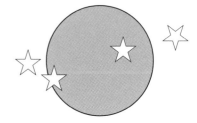

On St. Patrick's Day, the warm side of a stone turns up, and the broad-back goose begins to lay.

Secrets of the Zodiac

PISCES

FEBRUARY 20–MARCH 20

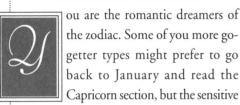

You are the romantic dreamers of the zodiac. Some of you more go-getter types might prefer to go back to January and read the Capricorn section, but the sensitive ones can stay here (there are two distinct types of Pisces). You have the ability to visit the Muses and bring back a fine creativity.

Unlike the other signs of the zodiac, you possess no singular energy of your own; rather, you are a combination of all the signs. Because you have an overwhelming desire to merge consciously or unconsciously, you intuit what others need from you, and you act accordingly. The compassion and understanding that is your ultimate gift can sometimes be problematic until you have learned how to define yourself.

Because of your sensitivity, you should always have a room of your own. You need regularly scheduled "alone time" and should be encouraged to learn how to say no. Your world is full of imagination and fantasy, so a creative outlet is also a must.

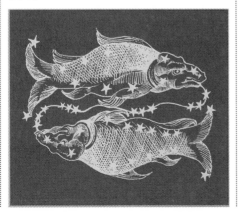

GOT A RUN?

■ Don't toss out your old ruined pantyhose. Wash them and put them to work . . .

- as a temporary substitute for a broken fan belt in your car.

- as a soap mitt—just fill a section with scraps of soap and tie off the ends.

- as ties to secure plants to garden stakes—simply cut the pantyhose into strips.

- as a bag to store Vidalia onions—tie the pantyhose in a knot above each onion so that the onions don't touch each other.

TEMPERATURE CONVERSION FORMULA

Fahrenheit to Celsius

To convert temperatures from Fahrenheit to Celsius, subtract 32 and multiply by .5556 (or $\frac{5}{9}$).
Example: (50°F - 32) x .5556 = 10°C

Celsius to Fahrenheit

To convert temperatures from Celsius to Fahrenheit, multiply by 1.8 (or $\frac{9}{5}$) and add 32.
Example: (30°C x 1.8) + 32 = 86°F

Cricket Chirps to Temperature

To convert cricket chirps to degrees Fahrenheit: Count the number of chirps in 14 seconds, then add 40.
Example: 30 chirps + 40 = 70°F

To convert cricket chirps to degrees Celsius: Count the number of chirps in 25 seconds, divide by 3, then add 4.
Example: (48 chirps ÷ 3) + 4 = 20°C

MARCH

1 | *Monday*

If you kill one flea in March, you'll kill a hundred.

---

2 | *Tuesday*

Texas Independence Day
Town Meeting Day (Vt.)

You must be the change you wish to see in the world.
–Mahatma Gandhi, Indian spiritual leader (1869–1948)

---

3 | *Wednesday*

Eat cabbage, avocados, and parsley to build strong bones.

---

4 | *Thursday*

Nick morning-glory seeds and plant in peat pots. Transplant outdoors after last frost.

MARCH • 2004

S	M	T	W	T	F	S
	1	2	3	4	5	6
7	8	9	10	11	12	13
14	15	16	17	18	19	20
21	22	23	24	25	26	27
28	29	30	31			

APRIL • 2004

S	M	T	W	T	F	S
				1	2	3
4	5	6	7	8	9	10
11	12	13	14	15	16	17
18	19	20	21	22	23	24
25	26	27	28	29	30	

Friday

5

**In calm water, every ship
has a good captain.**
–Swedish proverb

Saturday

6

Full Worm Moon

In March, birds begin
to search for worms.

Sunday

7

Buying in bulk saves
time and money.

SWEET CORN

FIELD CORN

REMINDERS

MARCH

8   *Monday*

Two days after the full
Moon is a good time
to plant or sow.

9   *Tuesday*

Fruit-juice ice cubes
keep a juice drink
cool and won't dilute
it as they melt.

10   *Wednesday*

Prune back rambler,
wild, and shrub roses
severely in spring.

11   *Thursday*

Unfinished
wood-handled tools
give fewer blisters.

MARCH • 2004							APRIL • 2004						
S	M	T	W	T	F	S	S	M	T	W	T	F	S
	1	2	3	4	5	6					1	2	3
7	8	9	10	11	12	13	4	5	6	7	8	9	10
14	15	16	17	18	19	20	11	12	13	14	15	16	17
21	22	23	24	25	26	27	18	19	20	21	22	23	24
28	29	30	31				25	26	27	28	29	30	

Deter deer from fruit trees by hanging bar soap from the branches.

Friday 12

Last Quarter Moon

Saturday 13

Look twice before you leap.
–Charlotte Brontë, English writer (1816–1855)

For a homegrown filling for Easter baskets, start grass seeds on a sponge in a dish of water.

Sunday 14

REMINDERS

March

15 *Monday*

Andrew Jackson Day (Tenn.)
Ides of March

*One man with courage
makes a majority.*
–Andrew Jackson, seventh
U.S. president (1767–1845)

16 *Tuesday*

Always running out
of milk?
Homogenized milk
can be frozen.

17 *Wednesday*

St. Patrick's Day
Evacuation Day (Suffolk Co., Mass.)

Prune dead or
winter-damaged canes
of climbing, tea, and
tree roses now.

18 *Thursday*

Remove rust from
tinware with a
cut potato dipped in
baking soda or salt.

MARCH • 2004

S	M	T	W	T	F	S
	1	2	3	4	5	6
7	8	9	10	11	12	13
14	15	16	17	18	19	20
21	22	23	24	25	26	27
28	29	30	31			

APRIL • 2004

S	M	T	W	T	F	S
				1	2	3
4	5	6	7	8	9	10
11	12	13	14	15	16	17
18	19	20	21	22	23	24
25	26	27	28	29	30	

Friday **19**

**Dream of a hedgehog
and you'll see
an old friend soon.**

Saturday **20**

**Vernal Equinox
New Moon**

*Welcome hither,
As is the spring to th'
earth.*
–William Shakespeare, English
playwright (1564–1616)

Sunday **21**

Aries the Ram
(Mar. 21 to Apr. 20)
is childlike and
strong-willed.
Motto: "I am!"

REMINDERS

MARCH

22 Monday

How many things I can do without!
–Socrates, Greek philosopher
(469–399 B.C.)

23 Tuesday

Coconut-fiber baskets keep the roots of hanging plants cool and moist.

24 Wednesday

To whip cream more easily, add a pinch of salt.

25 Thursday

Annunciation

Is't on St. Mary's bright and clear,
Fertile is said to be the year.

MARCH • 2004   APRIL • 2004

S	M	T	W	T	F	S	S	M	T	W	T	F	S
	1	2	3	4	5	6					1	2	3
7	8	9	10	11	12	13	4	5	6	7	8	9	10
14	15	16	17	18	19	20	11	12	13	14	15	16	17
21	22	23	24	25	26	27	18	19	20	21	22	23	24
28	29	30	31				25	26	27	28	29	30	

Dip pruning shears in sterilized skim milk to prevent the spread of plant viruses.

Friday 26

Married when March winds
shrill and roar,
Your home will be on a
distant shore.

Saturday 27

First Quarter Moon

Sunday 28

Cut firewood during
this Moon phase.

REMINDERS

29 Monday

Save your milk jugs to make tomato hotcaps (mini greenhouses).

30 Tuesday

Bubbles floating on the surface of your tea suggest money in store.

31 Wednesday

Lettuce is like conversation: It must be fresh and crisp, so sparkling that you barely notice the bitter in it.
–Charles Dudley Warner, American editor (1829–1900)

1 Thursday

All Fools' Day

Providence protects children and idiots. I know because I have tested it.
–Mark Twain, American writer (1835–1910)

MARCH • 2004	APRIL • 2004

S	M	T	W	T	F	S
	1	2	3	4	5	6
7	8	9	10	11	12	13
14	15	16	17	18	19	20
21	22	23	24	25	26	27
28	29	30	31			

S	M	T	W	T	F	S
				1	2	3
4	5	6	7	8	9	10
11	12	13	14	15	16	17
18	19	20	21	22	23	24
25	26	27	28	29	30	

Pascua Florida Day

Friday

2

Dab a bee or wasp sting with a little ammonia to prevent swelling.

Fertilize daffodils when the first shoots appear.

Saturday

3

Palm Sunday
Daylight Saving Time begins at 2:00 A.M.

Sunday

4

A cold April, the barn will fill.

REMINDERS

APRIL

with *The Old Farmer's Almanac*

125 Years Ago

FARMER'S CALENDAR, APRIL 1879

*W*here land was laid down last fall, there may be a lot of little stones that ought to be picked up and carted off. The way that some have of piling them up in heaps and letting them lie there, is no way to do it. Get them off and be done with them. Sow clover-seed on fall-sown grasslands. We ought to grow more clover; it is one of the best crops on the farm; it leaves the soil better than it found it. Corn or wheat will do as well after a heavy clover crop, without manure, as they will after most other crops with it. The kitchen garden must have its full share of time now; let it be near the house. If it is too old, take up a new and larger lot. Dig it deep and make it rich with manure, put on in the fall so as to give it time to rot down and get well mixed in with the soil; or if you must put it on now, let it be old and fat with age. No crude stuff where you want to grow nice crops. They all take their food in a liquid form, you know, and it takes time to get it into shape. Pease ought to go in at once, and some of the roots and vegetables. Don't forget to have plenty of small fruits. Nothing better than currants; and strawberries are always toothsome.

—The Old Farmer's Almanac

FULL-MOON LORE

The Full Pink Moon occurs on April 5 in 2004. It is called the Pink Moon because of the wild ground phlox, one of the earliest widespread flowers of the spring, usually in bloom around this time. It is also often called the Sprouting Grass Moon.

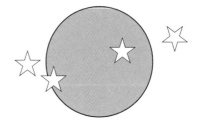

The dews of April
and May
Make August and
September gay.

Secrets of the Zodiac

ARIES

MARCH 21–APRIL 20

ou are the initiators of the zodiac. Dashing hither and yon (you are always in a hurry), you rush fearlessly ahead with little regard for your own safety. You like to be first in all that you do, and you are happiest when sharing your new discoveries with your friends. Willing to begin conversations with total strangers, you usually have many friends.

Generally optimistic, you often possess a bright, cheery smile that warms the hearts of those around you. While sometimes tactless, you are without guile, and what comes into the head slips right out of the mouth (unless Scorpio predominates elsewhere in your chart).

You should work in a job or career that allows you to pioneer something new or encourages you to be independent. You are very capable and will aim for the top. Boundless energy is yours, and you should get up and move around frequently or spend your lunches at the gym if you are chained to a desk.

HOMEMADE MOTH REPELLENT

This repellent is a nice change from mothballs.

1 handful each dried thyme, tansy, peppermint, pennyroyal, and whole cloves
2 handfuls each dried lavender, southernwood, santolina, and lemon rind
1 tablespoon powdered orrisroot
several drops lemon or clove oil

■ Combine all the ingredients and spoon into cheesecloth or cotton bags, filling each bag with about ½ cup repellent. Hang the bags in closets or over hangers that hold your woolens.

DID YOU HEAR THAT?

■ Decibels (dB) are used to measure the loudness, or intensity, of sounds. One decibel is the smallest difference between sounds detectable by the human ear. Intensity varies exponentially: A 20-dB sound is 10 times louder than a 10-dB sound; a 30-dB sound is 100 times louder than a 10-dB sound; a 40-dB sound is 1,000 times louder than a 10-dB sound; and so on. A 120-dB sound is painful.

10 decibels	*Light whisper*
20	*Quiet conversation*
30	*Normal conversation*
40	*Light traffic*
50	*Loud conversation*
60	*Noisy office*
70	*Normal traffic, quiet train*
80	*Rock music, subway*
90	*Heavy traffic, thunder*
100	*Jet plane at takeoff*

April

5 *Monday*

Full Pink Moon

Gather "spring tonic"
greens now:
fiddleheads, dandelion
greens, leeks.

6 *Tuesday*

First day of Passover

*Give your own opinion
of people, . . . but never
repeat that of others.*
—Ladies Indispensable
Assistant, 1852

7 *Wednesday*

Want to lose weight?
Eat pineapple to help
digest proteins and fat.

8 *Thursday*

Plant lettuce and
spinach in wide rows
(not single lines) to
delay bolting.

APRIL • 2004

S	M	T	W	T	F	S
				1	2	3
4	5	6	7	8	9	10
11	12	13	14	15	16	17
18	19	20	21	22	23	24
25	26	27	28	29	30	

MAY • 2004

S	M	T	W	T	F	S
						1
2	3	4	5	6	7	8
9	10	11	12	13	14	15
16	17	18	19	20	21	22
23	24	25	26	27	28	29
30	31					

Good Friday

Friday 9

Preserve the egg laid
on Good Friday and it will
safeguard your flock.

Saturday 10

Flossing and brushing,
besides being good
dental hygiene,
may increase your
longevity.

Easter
Orthodox Easter
Last Quarter Moon

Sunday 11

Rain on Easter, rain for
seven Sundays.

REMINDERS

APRIL

12 *Monday*   Easter Monday

Broken zipper pull?
Replace it with a
paper clip.

13 *Tuesday*   Thomas Jefferson's Birthday

*. . . although an old
man, I am but a
young gardener.*
–Thomas Jefferson (at age
68), third U.S. president
(1743–1826)

14 *Wednesday*   **A sunshiny shower
lasts half an hour.**

15 *Thursday*   Use an old wheeled
golf bag to tote
garden tools around.

APRIL • 2004

S	M	T	W	T	F	S
				1	2	3
4	5	6	7	8	9	10
11	12	13	14	15	16	17
18	19	20	21	22	23	24
25	26	27	28	29	30	

MAY • 2004

S	M	T	W	T	F	S
						1
2	3	4	5	6	7	8
9	10	11	12	13	14	15
16	17	18	19	20	21	22
23	24	25	26	27	28	29
30	31					

Soak dried herbs in
olive oil to enhance
flavor.

Friday **16**

Married beneath April's
changing skies,
A checkered path before
you lies.

Saturday **17**

The wind in one's face
[adversity] makes one wise.

Sunday **18**

REMINDERS

APRIL

19 *Monday*

Patriots Day (Maine; Mass.)
New Moon

Dandelion blossoms close
before a rain.

20 *Tuesday*

The second day of the
new Moon is propitious for
buying or selling.

21 *Wednesday*

San Jacinto Day (Tex.)

Taurus's stalwart Bull
(Apr. 21 to May 20)
states, "I have."

22 *Thursday*

Earth Day

Root crops and
asparagus will thrive
with an application
of seaweed dug into
the soil.

	APRIL • 2004							MAY • 2004					
S	M	T	W	T	F	S	S	M	T	W	T	F	S
				1	2	3							1
4	5	6	7	8	9	10	2	3	4	5	6	7	8
11	12	13	14	15	16	17	9	10	11	12	13	14	15
18	19	20	21	22	23	24	16	17	18	19	20	21	22
25	26	27	28	29	30		23	24	25	26	27	28	29
							30	31					

St. George's Day (N.L., Can.)

Friday 23

St. George cries "Goe!"
St. Mark [Apr. 25] cries "Hoe!"

Saturday 24

The Old Farmer's Almanac founder, Robert B. Thomas, was born on this day in 1766.

Sunday 25

Life is for one generation; a good name is forever.
–Japanese proverb

REMINDERS

APRIL ❦ MAY

26 *Monday*

Ease a headache by drinking tomato juice blended with fresh basil.

27 *Tuesday*

Apply boiled linseed oil to dried tool handles.

28 *Wednesday*

When the wild shadbush blooms, look for shad to run.

29 *Thursday*

If you spot an earwig when you go fishing, you'll have good luck.

APRIL • 2004

S	M	T	W	T	F	S
				1	2	3
4	5	6	7	8	9	10
11	12	13	14	15	16	17
18	19	20	21	22	23	24
25	26	27	28	29	30	

MAY • 2004

S	M	T	W	T	F	S
						1
2	3	4	5	6	7	8
9	10	11	12	13	14	15
16	17	18	19	20	21	22
23	24	25	26	27	28	29
30	31					

National Arbor Day

Friday **30**

Adding a new tree? Line the planting hole with newspapers to keep the root ball moist.

May Day

Saturday **1**

Hoarfrost today indicates a good harvest.

Married when bees over May blossoms flit,
Strangers around your board will sit.

Sunday **2**

REMINDERS

MAY

with The Old Farmer's Almanac

125 Years Ago

FARMER'S CALENDAR, MAY 1879

With all the hurry of this merry month, don't forget to set out a few fruit-trees. The time is coming when we are going to have peaches again, and every farmer ought to try his luck by setting out a few trees every year. Give them a northern or eastern slope where a warm spell in winter will not start the buds. The old time for turning the cows to pasture was the twentieth, but it was too late. It is best for the cows and best for the grass to get them out early, as soon as there is a fresh bite. Two or three hours a day will do at first, and keep up the feed in the barn at the same time. Make the change slowly, so that they will not lose a relish for hay. If you wait till the grass starts all over the pasture, and then turn in the cows, they reject the rank growth and it runs up to seed. They will not touch it; while if they had a nip at it when it first started, they would have kept it down. The short blade is the sweetest. Sow mangolds about the tenth. Get corn in early, and sow sweet corn every ten days, so as to have a supply for the table. Carrot seed ought to go in by the middle of the month. Don't fail to set out a lot of asparagus; it is one of the best things we have.

–The Old Farmer's Almanac

FULL-MOON LORE

The Full Flower Moon occurs on May 4 in 2004. Flowers spring forth in abundance this month. Some Algonquin tribes knew this Moon as the Corn Planting Moon or the Milk Moon.

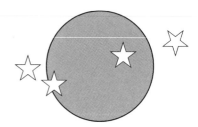

A misty May and a hot June
Bring cheap meal and harvest soon.

Secrets of the Zodiac

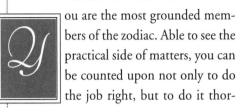

TAURUS

APRIL 21–MAY 20

ou are the most grounded members of the zodiac. Able to see the practical side of matters, you can be counted upon not only to do the job right, but to do it thoroughly as well. Although it may sometimes take you a while to gain momentum, your gift is the determination and persistence that carries you along once you have begun.

Your most basic need is for security; this is why it is so important for you to have your name on the deed somewhere. You like to build upon that which has already been established, and a firm home life makes it possible for you to go out and accomplish much in the workplace.

Known for your ability to spot bargains, you nevertheless go for quality rather than quantity. Often possessing a green thumb, you have the ability to make things grow and a need to feel connected to the earth. Walking barefoot or having somebody rub your feet can always bring you back to center when you begin to feel unbalanced.

SOIL MIX FOR CONTAINERS

1 part peat moss
1 part rich garden soil or potting soil
1 part sand

■ With a hoe or trowel, mix ingredients in a bucket, tub, or wheelbarrow until well blended. Use for outdoor potted vegetables or flowers.

FLOWERS*
THAT
ATTRACT
HUMMINGBIRDS

Beard tongue . . . . *Penstemon*
Bee balm . . . . *Monarda*
Butterfly bush. . . . . *Buddleia*
Columbine . . . . *Aquilegia*
Coral bells . . . . *Heuchera*
Daylily . . . . *Hemerocallis*
Desert candle. . . . . *Yucca*
Flag iris . . . . *Iris*
Flowering tobacco . . . . *Nicotiana alata*
Foxglove . . . . *Digitalis*
Larkspur . . . . *Delphinium*
Lily . . . . *Lilium*
Lupine . . . . *Lupinus*
Petunia . . . . *Petunia*
Red-hot poker. . . . . *Kniphofia*
Scarlet sage . . . . *Salvia splendens*
Summer phlox . . . . *Phlox paniculata*
Trumpet honeysuckle . . . . *Lonicera*
sempervirens
Verbena . . . . *Verbena*
Weigela. *Weigela*

*Note: Choose varieties in red and orange shades.

MAY

3 Monday

Never read a book that
is not a year old.
–Ralph Waldo Emerson,
American writer (1803–1882)

4 Tuesday

Full Flower Moon

If flowers stay open at night,
the next day will be wet.

5 Wednesday

Cinco de Mayo

Do a word jumble
or crossword puzzle;
exercising your mind
slows mental aging.

Look for striped
bass when dogwoods
bloom.

6 Thursday

MAY • 2004

S	M	T	W	T	F	S
						1
2	3	4	5	6	7	8
9	10	11	12	13	14	15
16	17	18	19	20	21	22
23	24	25	26	27	28	29
30	31					

JUNE • 2004

S	M	T	W	T	F	S
		1	2	3	4	5
6	7	8	9	10	11	12
13	14	15	16	17	18	19
20	21	22	23	24	25	26
27	28	29	30			

Friday

7

The Aztecs said that tree and flower scents would cure "lassitude" in "those holding public office."

Truman Day (Mo.)

Saturday

8

If you can't convince them, confuse them.

–Harry S. Truman, 33rd U.S. president (1884–1972)

Mother's Day

Sunday

9

Plant a gift window box of pansies, silver-leaved sage, and yarrow.

REMINDERS

MAY

10   *Monday*

Spill your face powder
and you will quarrel with
a friend.

11   *Tuesday*

Last Quarter Moon

The Three Chilly Saints
bring cold weather on May
11, 12, and 13.

12   *Wednesday*

Brush the dog and
twine the fur into the
garden fence to ward
off critters.

13   *Thursday*

*Opportunity is missed
by most people because
it is dressed in overalls
and looks like work.*
–Thomas Edison, American
inventor (1847–1931)

MAY • 2004

S M T W T F S
                1
2 3 4 5 6 7 8
9 10 11 12 13 14 15
16 17 18 19 20 21 22
23 24 25 26 27 28 29
30 31

JUNE • 2004

S M T W T F S
      1 2 3 4 5
6 7 8 9 10 11 12
13 14 15 16 17 18 19
20 21 22 23 24 25 26
27 28 29 30

Friday

14

If you would be happy
your whole life long, become
a gardener.
—Chinese proverb

Saturday

15

Armed Forces Day

*I do love
My country's good with
a respect more tender,
More holy and
profound, than mine
own life.*
—William Shakespeare, English
playwright (1564–1616)

Sunday

16

Dandruff? Beat an
egg white and use it
to cleanse the scalp.
Rinse well.

REMINDERS

MAY

17 *Monday*

*. . . my heart with
pleasure fills
And dances with the
daffodils.*
–William Wordsworth,
English poet (1770–1850)

18 *Tuesday*

An upside-down
flag is considered a
distress signal.

19 *Wednesday*

New Moon

Grapes and raisins
contain low levels of
pain relievers, good
for arthritis.

20 *Thursday*

Plant pole beans
and bush beans away
from onions; they're
incompatible.

MAY • 2004   JUNE • 2004

S M T W T F S   S M T W T F S
                  1   1 2 3 4 5
2 3 4 5 6 7 8   6 7 8 9 10 11 12
9 10 11 12 13 14 15   13 14 15 16 17 18 19
16 17 18 19 20 21 22   20 21 22 23 24 25 26
23 24 25 26 27 28 29   27 28 29 30
30 31

Gemini's mutable
Twins (May 21 to
June 20) say,
"I communicate."

Friday 21

National Maritime Day

Knitting hair into the
toe of a sailor's sock
was said to bring him
home safely.

Saturday 22

For dried cut flowers,
plant globe thistle,
lavender, money
plant, pearly
everlasting, and
yarrow.

Sunday 23

REMINDERS

Complement this calendar with daily weather and Almanac wit and wisdom at www.almanac.com.

May

24 *Monday*

Victoria Day (Canada)

Plant a crab-apple
tree for jelly or for
the birds.

25 *Tuesday*

*All who joy would win
Must share it,—
happiness was born
a twin.*

–Lord Byron, English poet
(1788–1824)

26 *Wednesday*

Add rock salt to the
asparagus bed to
increase production
(1 pound per 100
square feet).

27 *Thursday*

First Quarter Moon

Go plant the bean when the
Moon is light [waxing],
And you will find that this
is right.

MAY • 2004

S	M	T	W	T	F	S
						1
2	3	4	5	6	7	8
9	10	11	12	13	14	15
16	17	18	19	20	21	22
23	24	25	26	27	28	29
30	31					

JUNE • 2004

S	M	T	W	T	F	S
		1	2	3	4	5
6	7	8	9	10	11	12
13	14	15	16	17	18	19
20	21	22	23	24	25	26
27	28	29	30			

Friday **28**

*If you have leisure,
examine your fences.*

–The [Old] Farmer's
Almanac, 1801

Saturday **29**

*Hide not your talents.
They for use were
made. What's a sundial
in the shade?*

–Benjamin Franklin,
American statesman
(1706–1790)

Sunday **30**

𝔚𝔥𝔦𝔱𝔰𝔲𝔫𝔡𝔞𝔶–𝔓𝔢𝔫𝔱𝔢𝔠𝔬𝔰𝔱
𝔒𝔯𝔱𝔥𝔬𝔡𝔬𝔵 𝔓𝔢𝔫𝔱𝔢𝔠𝔬𝔰𝔱

Lilacs bloom on
year-old wood; prune
just after bloom.

REMINDERS

31 Monday

Memorial Day (observed)

Four be the things I am wiser to know: Idleness, sorrow, a friend, and a foe.
–Dorothy Parker, American writer (1893–1967)

1 Tuesday

Cut irises and peonies when buds show their first color.

2 Wednesday

When black locusts bloom, blue crabs will molt.

3 Thursday

Full Strawberry Moon

Rabbits hate the smell of rotted hay; use it to mulch strawberries.

May • 2004

S	M	T	W	T	F	S
						1
2	3	4	5	6	7	8
9	10	11	12	13	14	15
16	17	18	19	20	21	22
23	24	25	26	27	28	29
30	31					

June • 2004

S	M	T	W	T	F	S
		1	2	3	4	5
6	7	8	9	10	11	12
13	14	15	16	17	18	19
20	21	22	23	24	25	26
27	28	29	30			

**June damp and warm,
Does the farmer no harm.**

Friday

4

World Environment Day

Saturday

5

Native Americans recommended eating strawberries to prevent fainting.

Cut back Japanese rose shrubs *(Kerria japonica)* to the ground after flowering.

Sunday

6

REMINDERS

JUNE

with *The Old Farmer's Almanac*

125 Years Ago

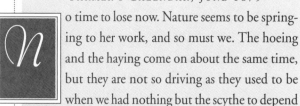

o time to lose now. Nature seems to be springing to her work, and so must we. The hoeing and the haying come on about the same time, but they are not so driving as they used to be when we had nothing but the scythe to depend upon. We can cut an acre an hour now; but when I was a boy, it took a man a day. This gives us time to keep up with the weeds, and it is a great gain. We have gained all of two weeks over the old style of work; that is, we cut grass two weeks earlier, and it is all the better for it. Early-cut hay, or dried grass, is far better for cows than the hay they used to get. Grasses are best cut in the bloom. If we sow only the early grasses together, and the late grasses by themselves, we spread the labor over a longer season. Sow orchard grass, tall oat-grass, June grass, and clover, and you can cut as early as the middle of this month. Then timothy, red-top, fine top, and tall oat-grass will make a mixture to cut later, say after the 4th of July. The swede is to be sown this month, soon after the 20th. Hungarian grass-seed ought to go in about the middle of the month; it is one of the very best forage crops.

–The Old Farmer's Almanac

FULL-MOON LORE

The Full Strawberry Moon occurs on June 3 in 2004. Algonquin tribes celebrated this Moon as a time to gather ripening fruit. This Moon is also known as the Rose Moon and the Hot Moon.

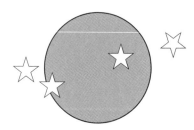

When the rainbow does not reach down to the water, clear weather will follow.

Secrets of the Zodiac

GEMINI

MAY 21–JUNE 20

You are the witty communicators of the zodiac. Words trip lightly off your tongue under any and all circumstances. You possess natural gifts for writing and speaking and are often drawn into fields where you can express your abilities.

Like your ruling planet, you are mercurial. You have a strong need for diversity and bore easily. In choosing a life path, you would do best to find an occupation that contains many different parts, as well as something that would allow you to move around. Many of you are found throughout journalism because this career satisfies your needs while allowing you also to emphasize your talents.

You love being part of your local community, and you can be counted upon to know and pass along most of the current gossip. Friends use you as a resource when seeking information about a particular service or product. You enjoy being cheerful, and you search for the lightness in all things.

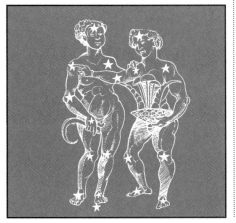

GARLIC BUG SPRAY

3 to 5 cloves garlic
2 cups water
1 teaspoon dish detergent

■ Combine ingredients in a blender and mix at high speed for 3 minutes. Strain through cheesecloth or a fine strainer, reserving garlic bits in a jar with a tight-fitting lid. Pour strained liquid into a spray bottle, and apply to flowers or vegetables before or during an insect invasion. (Apply in the early morning or late afternoon and after rain.) Add water to reserved garlic bits and store in the refrigerator. Use this mixture for a second batch.

WHAT'S IN A NAME?

■ The World Meteorological Organization (WMO) maintains regional lists of names for tropical cyclones worldwide, to facilitate the exchange of information about a particular storm. For especially severe storms, the WMO may retire and replace names.

When a disturbance near the United States intensifies into a tropical storm—with rotary circulation and wind speeds above 39 miles per hour—the National Hurricane Center near Miami, Florida, assigns it a name from the current year's list. The series of lists for the Atlantic and eastern North Pacific rotate over a six-year cycle.

2004 ATLANTIC TROPICAL-CYCLONE NAMES

Alex	Earl	Jeanne	Nicole	Tomas
Bonnie	Frances	Karl	Otto	Virginie
Charley	Gaston	Lisa	Paula	Walter
Danielle	Hermine	Matthew	Richard	
	Ivan		Shary	

JUNE

7 *Monday*

Forgot your asthma medicine? Caffeinated coffee may help.

8 *Tuesday*

Hyssop and radishes make poor garden companions.

9 *Wednesday*

Last Quarter Moon

Use the waning Moon to help quit smoking and complete old projects.

10 *Thursday*

Bury wood ashes around your fruit trees now.

JUNE • 2004

S	M	T	W	T	F	S
		1	2	3	4	5
6	7	8	9	10	11	12
13	14	15	16	17	18	19
20	21	22	23	24	25	26
27	28	29	30			

JULY • 2004

S	M	T	W	T	F	S
				1	2	3
4	5	6	7	8	9	10
11	12	13	14	15	16	17
18	19	20	21	22	23	24
25	26	27	28	29	30	31

Friday **11**

King Kamehameha I Day
(Hawaii)

On St. Barnabas' Day (today),
the Sun is come to stay.

Saturday **12**

Speak wedding vows on the
upward strokes of the clock
hands and you'll work well
together in marriage.

Sunday **13**

Build and maintain
friendships to increase
longevity.

REMINDERS

JUNE

14 *Monday* — Flag Day

Indoors, display the flag to the right of center stage as you face the audience.

15 *Tuesday*

Crushed bee balm or calendula leaves will ease a bee sting.

16 *Wednesday*

Gardens are not made by sitting in the shade.
–Rudyard Kipling, English writer (1865–1936)

17 *Thursday* — Bunker Hill Day (Suffolk Co., Mass.) / New Moon

. . . time to look about for pea-sticks and bean-poles.
–The [Old] Farmer's Almanac, 1801

JUNE • 2004

S	M	T	W	T	F	S
		1	2	3	4	5
6	7	8	9	10	11	12
13	14	15	16	17	18	19
20	21	22	23	24	25	26
27	28	29	30			

JULY • 2004

S	M	T	W	T	F	S
				1	2	3
4	5	6	7	8	9	10
11	12	13	14	15	16	17
18	19	20	21	22	23	24
25	26	27	28	29	30	31

If cumulus clouds are smaller at sunset than at noon, expect fair weather.

Friday 18

Emancipation Day (Tex.)

Saturday 19

Sunflowers bring good luck to the entire garden.

Father's Day
Summer Solstice

Sunday 20

Steep thyself in a bowl of summertime.
–Virgil, Roman poet
(70–19 B.C.)

REMINDERS

JUNE

21 *Monday*

The motto for Cancer's Crab (June 21 to July 22), "I feel," reflects the unconscious.

22 *Tuesday*

If you cut thistles before St. John's Day (June 24), they will double.

23 *Wednesday*

Midsummer Eve (today) was sacred to lovers.

24 *Thursday*

Fête Nationale (Que., Can.)
Discovery Day (N.L., Can.)

Rub crushed lemon thyme or lemon balm on your skin as an insect repellent.

JUNE • 2004

S	M	T	W	T	F	S
		1	2	3	4	5
6	7	8	9	10	11	12
13	14	15	16	17	18	19
20	21	22	23	24	25	26
27	28	29	30			

JULY • 2004

S	M	T	W	T	F	S
				1	2	3
4	5	6	7	8	9	10
11	12	13	14	15	16	17
18	19	20	21	22	23	24
25	26	27	28	29	30	31

First Quarter Moon

Friday **25**

Feed peonies when
their petals fall.

Married in the month of
roses—June,
Life will be one long
honeymoon.

Saturday **26**

*Happiness makes up in
height for what it lacks
in length.*
–Robert Frost, American poet
(1874–1963)

Sunday **27**

REMINDERS

JUNE ❦ JULY

28 *Monday*

Distinctive perfumes
come from plain
flowers.

29 *Tuesday*

Don't fertilize dry
soil. Water the soil
first, add fertilizer,
and water again.

30 *Wednesday*

*Why should a man die,
when he can go to his
garden for sage?*
–Tenth-century saying

1 *Thursday*

Canada Day

*Having dressed
yourself, pay no further
attention to your
clothes.*
*–Ladies Indispensable
Assistant, 1852*

JUNE • 2004

S	M	T	W	T	F	S
		1	2	3	4	5
6	7	8	9	10	11	12
13	14	15	16	17	18	19
20	21	22	23	24	25	26
27	28	29	30			

JULY • 2004

S	M	T	W	T	F	S
				1	2	3
4	5	6	7	8	9	10
11	12	13	14	15	16	17
18	19	20	21	22	23	24
25	26	27	28	29	30	31

Full Buck Moon

Friday

2

If animals crowd together, rain will follow.

As the Dog Days (traditionally hot and sultry) commence today, so they end (Aug. 11).

Saturday

3

Independence Day

Sunday

4

All serious daring starts from within.
–Eudora Welty, American writer (1909–2001)

REMINDERS

JULY

with *The Old Farmer's Almanac*

125 Years Ago

FARMER'S CALENDAR, JULY 1879

*I*t is of no use to grow bushes and weeds in the place where the grass ought to grow. It should be the aim of good farming to keep them down. As soon as the grass is cut, and the hay in the barn, let us turn to and put an end to them. Here is an old wall that is choked up with wild shrubs. Might as well get it out of the way. It was built before the mowing-machine was thought of, and it isn't just the thing for our style of work. Let us plan to till less ground and do it better. Do no more than you can do well. The best of work is none too good for the farm. Thrift comes from just that kind of work, so let us do our level best. Weeds must live on what we may call the food of plants. If the land is rich, they draw hard on it with their rank growth. Now, plant-food costs a great deal of time and money. We save it under the barn; we buy it at a high cost, brought as it is from long distances, and put it on the land to grow crops. We must take care not to be robbed of it by plants that we do not want. If we have a hive of busy bees, we try to guard them against theft. Why not do as much for the crops, and keep down the weeds? After haying, let us up and at them.

—The Old Farmer's Almanac

FULL-MOON LORE

The Full Buck Moon occurs on July 2 in 2004, and is so named because this is the time when bucks begin growing antlers. Another name for a July Moon is the Thunder Moon, assigned this year to the full Moon occurring on July 31. The second full Moon in a month is sometimes called a blue Moon.

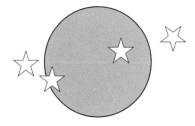

In the decay of the Moon,
A cloudy morning bodes
a fair afternoon.

Secrets of the Zodiac

CANCER

JUNE 21–JULY 22

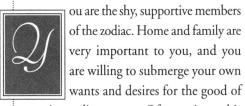

ou are the shy, supportive members of the zodiac. Home and family are very important to you, and you are willing to submerge your own wants and desires for the good of your immediate group. Often quite ambitious, you seek to get ahead in order to provide the best for your loved ones.

Like your animal, the crab, your tough exterior hides a very soft interior. You take everything to heart; though you may not show it, you are easily wounded. You feel experiences intensely, and you bring this knowledge into your relationships with others. Gentle and caring, you are always ready to lend an ear or make another a cup of tea.

You often possess extraordinary culinary abilities, and your meals, though delicious, are also quite nutritious. In choosing a profession, you would do well to pick an occupation that gives you an opportunity to express the compassion that you feel for others. You are loyal and patriotic, and employers can be sure of your personal devotion.

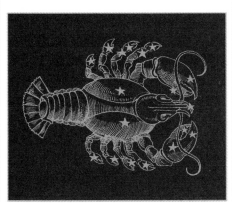

MOSS FRAPPÉ

½ cup garden moss
1 cup buttermilk

■ Combine ingredients in a blender, and mix at medium speed until smooth. Sprinkle mixture over a prepared soil bed, and moss will grow there.

TRANSPLANTING JUICE

1 package dry yeast
2 gallons warm water

■ Combine ingredients in a watering can, and stir until yeast dissolves. Use to water newly transplanted vegetable or flower seedlings.

HERBS TO PLANT IN LAWNS

■ Choose plants that suit your soil and your climate. All these can withstand mowing and considerable foot traffic.

Ajuga or bugleweed *(Ajuga reptans)*
Corsican mint *(Mentha requienii)*
Dwarf cinquefoil *(Potentilla tabernaemontani)*
English pennyroyal *(Mentha pulegium)*
Green Irish moss *(Sagina subulata)*
Pearly everlasting *(Anaphalis margaritacea)*
Roman chamomile *(Chamaemelum nobile)*
Rupturewort *(Herniaria glabra)*
Speedwell *(Veronica officinalis)*
Stonecrop *(Sedum ternatum)*
Sweet violets *(Viola odorata* or *V. tricolor)*
Thyme *(Thymus serpyllum)*
White clover *(Trifolium repens)*
Wild strawberries *(Fragaria virginiana)*
Wintergreen or partridgeberry *(Mitchella repens)*

July

5 *Monday*

Choose coneflowers, daisies, marigolds, and zinnias for hot, dry rooftop or balcony gardens.

6 *Tuesday*

Wedding "bomboniera," or packets of sugared almonds, symbolize health, happiness, and fertility.

7 *Wednesday*

Keep cukes picked or the plants will stop producing.

8 *Thursday*

For sunburned skin, apply aloe vera straight from the plant.

JULY • 2004

S	M	T	W	T	F	S
				1	2	3
4	5	6	7	8	9	10
11	12	13	14	15	16	17
18	19	20	21	22	23	24
25	26	27	28	29	30	31

AUGUST • 2004

S	M	T	W	T	F	S
1	2	3	4	5	6	7
8	9	10	11	12	13	14
15	16	17	18	19	20	21
22	23	24	25	26	27	28
29	30	31				

Friday 9

Last Quarter Moon

Sprinkle cabbages
(when they are
wet) with rye flour
to discourage
cabbageworms.

Saturday 10

Saturdays are propitious
for setting sail. Fridays
are unlucky.

Sunday 11

Strawberries, high
in boron, fight
osteoporosis and
arthritis.

REMINDERS

July

12 Monday

Orangemen's Day (N.L., Can.)

**The gift of an orange
brings good luck.**

13 Tuesday

Balsam tips pocketed
for a few days smell
of strawberries,
according to Henry
David Thoreau.

14 Wednesday

To cure hiccups, take
anything that will
make you sneeze.

15 Thursday

St. Swithin's Day (today),
an ye be fair,
For forty days 'twill rain
nae mair.
–Scottish proverb

JULY • 2004

S	M	T	W	T	F	S
				1	2	3
4	5	6	7	8	9	10
11	12	13	14	15	16	17
18	19	20	21	22	23	24
25	26	27	28	29	30	31

AUGUST • 2004

S	M	T	W	T	F	S
1	2	3	4	5	6	7
8	9	10	11	12	13	14
15	16	17	18	19	20	21
22	23	24	25	26	27	28
29	30	31				

Friday 16

Reduce slug damage
by watering lettuce in
the morning instead
of at night.

Saturday 17

New Moon

Milkweed pods close
before a rain.

Sunday 18

When cleaning the
aquarium, use the old
water as plant food.

REMINDERS

July

19 *Monday*

Superior people never make long visits.
–Marianne Moore, American poet (1887–1972)

20 *Tuesday*

Crushed eggshells, when placed in thick rings around plants, deter slugs.

21 *Wednesday*

Nectarines, peaches, avocados, and tomatoes ripen faster in a closed paper bag at room temperature.

22 *Thursday*

Rose, rose and clematis, Trail and twine and clasp and kiss.
–Alfred, Lord Tennyson, English poet (1809–1892)

JULY • 2004   AUGUST • 2004

S M T W T F S   S M T W T F S
        1 2 3   1 2 3 4 5 6 7
4 5 6 7 8 9 10   8 9 10 11 12 13 14
11 12 13 14 15 16 17   15 16 17 18 19 20 21
18 19 20 21 22 23 24   22 23 24 25 26 27 28
25 26 27 28 29 30 31   29 30 31

Leo the Lion
(July 23 to Aug. 22),
fixed and dependable,
says, "I create."

Friday **23**

Pioneer Day (Utah)
First Quarter Moon

Saturday **24**

Travel makes a wise man
better but a fool worse.

Married in July with
flowers ablaze,
Bittersweet memories on
after days.

Sunday **25**

REMINDERS

July ❦ August

26 *Monday*

Feed container plants
twice a month with
liquid fertilizer.

27 *Tuesday*

**It is considered unlucky to
marry on your birthday.**

28 *Wednesday*

Sow beans for pickling.
–*The [Old] Farmer's
Almanac*, 1801

29 *Thursday*

For grease spills on
brick or cement:
Apply cornmeal, leave
it for a few hours, and
then sweep.

JULY • 2004

S	M	T	W	T	F	S
				1	2	3
4	5	6	7	8	9	10
11	12	13	14	15	16	17
18	19	20	21	22	23	24
25	26	27	28	29	30	31

AUGUST • 2004

S	M	T	W	T	F	S
1	2	3	4	5	6	7
8	9	10	11	12	13	14
15	16	17	18	19	20	21
22	23	24	25	26	27	28
29	30	31				

Walnut boughs or foxglove leaves repel fleas.

Friday 30

Full Thunder Moon

Saturday 31

This second full Moon of the month is known as a blue Moon.

After Lammas (today), corn ripens as much by night as by day.

Sunday 1

REMINDERS

AUGUST

with *The Old Farmer's Almanac*

125 Years Ago

FARMER'S CALENDAR, AUGUST 1879

Grass is the great crop with us, and it must be so for all time. To keep cows well through the year, with a long spell of cold weather which is sure to come, is the great problem we have to solve, and so we might as well bend all our plans to that. Now that the haying is over, let us see how we can lay out to cut more grass next year. More grass will keep more stock, more stock will give us more plant-food; more plant-food will keep up the land and give us some crop to sell. Top-dress the mowing lots; it is a good time to do it now. A compost heap, with muck and lime, ashes and bone-meal, is just what the field wants, and the more of it the better. Stiff loam makes a good basis for a grass compost for light land; and if we add some nitrate of soda, or what is called the Chili saltpetre of commerce, and a few German potash salts, it will pay in the end. Why not get out a lot of clay or loam and use it in this way; put it under the sink-spout, and soak up all the waste water. Sow round turnips at once where the pease and the early potatoes grew. Dig ditches; it pays to drain the lowlands. Cut the bushes along the walls. Spruce up, as they say, and get ready for the fall work.

–The Old Farmer's Almanac

FULL-MOON LORE

The Full Sturgeon Moon occurs on August 29 in 2004. The sturgeon of the Great Lakes and Lake Champlain were most readily caught at this time. This Moon is also known as the Green Corn Moon and the Red Moon.

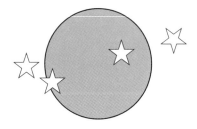

If the flowers keep open all night, the weather will be wet the next day.

Secrets of the Zodiac

LEO

JULY 23–AUGUST 22

You are the naturals of the zodiac. Unusually talented, you possess inherent abilities for which even you can't account. Often dazzlingly charming, you light up a room with your presence, and all in attendance know where you are. Your broad smile and bright eyes make others feel warm and welcome.

You always play to the audience. With dramatic effect, you tell your stories, pausing at the right places, occasionally gesturing for emphasis. You need to see a response. Some form of acknowledgment such as a pat on the back is as important to you as the air you breathe. You need to be noticed.

As your personality is strong, you prefer friends who can meet your strength. You seek positions of leadership in employment, and you do well as the head of a department or in business for yourself. As you think big, bold, bright, and beautiful, your dreams can carry you far.

KITCHEN COMPOST TEA

■ Fill an old blender with water to within a few inches of the top. Add about 1 cup of compostable kitchen garbage (vegetable peelings, coffee grounds, etc.). Mix at high speed until the organic matter is very fine and suspended in the water. Immediately use on container gardens or potted plants.

CLOUD DEFINITIONS

High Clouds (bases starting at about 20,000 feet)

Cirrus: Thin feather-like crystal clouds.

Cirrocumulus: Thin clouds that appear as small "cotton patches."

Cirrostratus: Thin white clouds that resemble veils.

Middle Clouds (bases starting at about 10,000 feet)

Altocumulus: Gray or white layer or patches of solid clouds with rounded shapes.

Altostratus: Grayish or bluish layer of clouds that can obscure the Sun.

Low Clouds (bases starting near Earth's surface to about 6,500 feet)

Stratus: Thin, gray sheet-like clouds with low bases; may bring drizzle and snow.

Stratocumulus: Rounded cloud masses that form on top of a layer.

Nimbostratus: Dark, gray shapeless cloud layers containing rain, snow, and ice pellets.

Clouds with Vertical Development (high clouds that form at almost any altitude and reach up to about 14,000 feet)

Cumulus: Fair-weather clouds with flat bases and domeshaped tops.

Cumulonimbus: Large, dark, vertical clouds with bulging tops that bring showers, thunder, and lightning.

AUGUST

2 *Monday*

Observe the first heavy fog of August and expect a frost that day in October.

3 *Tuesday*

Dry spots in the lawn? Replant with fragrant wild thyme.

4 *Wednesday*

Don't attitudenize.
—Dr. Samuel Johnson, English writer (1709–1784)

5 *Thursday*

Use acid-free paper and boxes to store a wedding dress or other valuable garments.

AUGUST • 2004

S	M	T	W	T	F	S
1	2	3	4	5	6	7
8	9	10	11	12	13	14
15	16	17	18	19	20	21
22	23	24	25	26	27	28
29	30	31				

SEPTEMBER • 2004

S	M	T	W	T	F	S
			1	2	3	4
5	6	7	8	9	10	11
12	13	14	15	16	17	18
19	20	21	22	23	24	25
26	27	28	29	30		

Friday 6

Going away? Run a few lemon wedges through the garbage disposal, then rinse, to avoid odors.

Saturday 7

Last Quarter Moon

Nibble lamb's-quarters raw or boiled like spinach.

Sunday 8

Sunshine—in moderation—is a mood enhancer and boosts immunity.

REMINDERS

AUGUST

9 *Monday*

Victory Day (R.I.)

**Clip witch-hazel twigs
and wear them in your hair
to get a wish.**

10 *Tuesday*

*Clear out ditches . . .
and cart the dirt into
your barnyards.*

—The [Old] Farmer's
Almanac, 1801

11 *Wednesday*

*A horse is dangerous
at both ends and
uncomfortable in the
middle.*

—Ian Fleming, English writer
(1908–1964)

12 *Thursday*

Inspect and repair
gutters now.

AUGUST • 2004

S	M	T	W	T	F	S
1	2	3	4	5	6	7
8	9	10	11	12	13	14
15	16	17	18	19	20	21
22	23	24	25	26	27	28
29	30	31				

SEPTEMBER • 2004

S	M	T	W	T	F	S
			1	2	3	4
5	6	7	8	9	10	11
12	13	14	15	16	17	18
19	20	21	22	23	24	25
26	27	28	29	30		

Friday 13

Every year has at
least one Friday the
13th and no more
than three. (This year
has two.)

Saturday 14

For insomnia,
rock gently or listen
to the sound of
running water.

New Moon

Sunday 15

Start slips for
houseplants at
August's new Moon.

REMINDERS

AUGUST

16 *Monday*
Bennington Battle Day (Vt.)
Discovery Day (Y.T., Can.)

*Action is the antidote
to despair.*
–Joan Baez, American singer
(b. 1941)

17 *Tuesday*
Cat Nights commence.

*Cats are inquisitive but
hate to admit it.*
–Mason Cooley, American
writer (b. 1927)

18 *Wednesday*
The best fishing
occurs between the
new (15th) and full
(29th) Moons.

19 *Thursday*
National Aviation Day

*Courage is the price
that life exacts for
granting peace.*
–Amelia Earhart, American
aviator (1897–1937)

S	M	T	W	T	F	S
1	2	3	4	5	6	7
8	9	10	11	12	13	14
15	16	17	18	19	20	21
22	23	24	25	26	27	28
29	30	31				

S	M	T	W	T	F	S
			1	2	3	4
5	6	7	8	9	10	11
12	13	14	15	16	17	18
19	20	21	22	23	24	25
26	27	28	29	30		

Friday **20**

Gather elderberries
when they're ripe and
have lost their sheen
but are not withered.

Saturday **21**

A parsley poultice
should clear up a
bruise within a day
or two.

Sunday **22**

Edible flowers
include begonias,
chive blossoms,
nasturtiums, and
violets.

REMINDERS

AUGUST

23 *Monday*

First Quarter Moon

Virgo's mutable
Virgin (Aug. 23 to
Sept. 22) has the
motto "I serve."

24 *Tuesday*

*A stale mind is the
devil's bread box.*
–Unknown

25 *Wednesday*

Refrigerated
tomatoes get mushy,
not ripe.

26 *Thursday*

Women's Equality Day

*Just remember, we're all
in this alone.*
–Lily Tomlin, American
actress (b. 1939)

AUGUST • 2004   SEPTEMBER • 2004

S	M	T	W	T	F	S
1	2	3	4	5	6	7
8	9	10	11	12	13	14
15	16	17	18	19	20	21
22	23	24	25	26	27	28
29	30	31				

S	M	T	W	T	F	S
			1	2	3	4
5	6	7	8	9	10	11
12	13	14	15	16	17	18
19	20	21	22	23	24	25
26	27	28	29	30		

Friday 27

Place a rain barrel under your gutter's downspout to save water for the garden.

Saturday 28

Married in August's heat and drowse,
Lover and friend in your chosen spouse.

Sunday 29

Full Sturgeon Moon

When corn fodder is crisp, fair weather.

REMINDERS

AUGUST ❧ SEPTEMBER

30 Monday

Breathing exercises and soothing music can ease flying fears.

31 Tuesday

To remove tarnish, wash brass in the water from boiled potatoes.

1 Wednesday

Drye roses put to ye nose to smell do comforte the brain.
–17th-century English herbal

2 Thursday

For customized stationery, press herb leaves onto a stamp pad, then onto paper.

AUGUST • 2004

S	M	T	W	T	F	S
1	2	3	4	5	6	7
8	9	10	11	12	13	14
15	16	17	18	19	20	21
22	23	24	25	26	27	28
29	30	31				

SEPTEMBER • 2004

S	M	T	W	T	F	S
			1	2	3	4
5	6	7	8	9	10	11
12	13	14	15	16	17	18
19	20	21	22	23	24	25
26	27	28	29	30		

Get frugal! Living beyond your means adds stress and reduces immunity.

Friday 3

Dry seed heads of Chinese lanterns, globe thistles, and poppies right side up.

Saturday 4

For playground safety, avoid necklaces and drawstrings on children's clothing.

Sunday 5

REMINDERS

September

with *The Old Farmer's Almanac*

125 Years Ago

I like to sow grass-seed in dog-days, if the land is moist enough; it has time then to start and get a good root by the time the cold comes to close the ground. It will stand the winter better than if it is sown later. You can't be too careful in laying down land; a smooth and mellow surface is needed. The seeds of grasses are very small: they must have a good seed-bed, or they will not grow. A light top-dressing, sown on after the seed, is worth more than it costs; it gives a quick and strong start, and helps the young grass-plants to keep ahead of the weeds. A roller is one of the best tools on the farm for laying down to grass; it leaves a smooth and even top, and presses down the seed so as to make it sprout well. It is time, too, to sow winter grains. Rye and wheat do well here, and they pay as well as most crops. Fall ploughing is in order now. All stiff or strong soils are better for early ploughing in the fall. The sod will rot and grow finer than it will if turned over in spring, and the weathering of winter is good for it. Pick out and mark the earliest and best ears of corn for seed while it still stands in the field. It is a fine time to cut timber for posts and rails.

–*The Old Farmer's Almanac*

FULL-MOON LORE

The Full Harvest Moon occurs on September 28 in 2004. The Harvest Moon is always the full Moon nearest the autumnal equinox, delivering more light in the early evening to aid in the harvest.

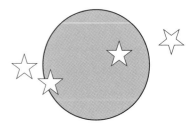

Clear autumn, windy winter;
Warm autumn, long winter.

Secrets of the Zodiac

Virgo

August 23–September 22

You are the organized thinkers of the zodiac. With a critical eye, you dissect and analyze all sorts of data. You are able to see instantly the flaw in any situation. Loving information, you file and store it away for future retrieval.

You do well in all sorts of scientific pursuits. Able to memorize infinite amounts of information, you love the study of phylums and dictums. Your organizational ability is particularly strong, and though your home and office may not always be as neat as a pin, you are aware of the placement of each and every one of your belongings. You desire life at the top, and you are well aware of the steps involved in getting there.

Incorporating a sense of humor into your personality keeps you from becoming overly serious. Dependable and responsible, you must guard against taking on the accountability of others. Once you have truly learned how to have fun, yours is an enviable life.

Cut-Flower Hints

■ Cut flowers last longest if their stems are cut with a sharp blade, either underwater or seconds before being plunged into water. The water should be warmish, never icy.

■ Keep cut flowers in a cool spot in water conditioned with packaged floral preservative or a homemade treatment of 1 tablespoon sugar and 1 tablespoon lemon juice or vinegar per quart of water.

■ To remove stains inside your glass vases, rub two to three tablespoons of salt onto the area, then scrub clean with a damp bristle brush.

Proper Canning Practices

■ Carefully select and wash fresh food.
■ Peel some fresh foods.
■ Hot-pack many foods.
■ Add acids (lemon juice or vinegar) to some foods.
■ Use acceptable jars and self-sealing lids.
■ Process jars in a pressure canner or a boiling-water canner for the correct amount of time.

Quantities Needed for Canning

Fruits	Vegetables
Quantity per Quart Canned (pounds)	*Quantity per Quart Canned (pounds)*
Apples . . . . 2½ to 3	Asparagus. . . . 2½ to 4½
Blackberries . . 1½ to 3½	Beans . . . . 1½ to 2½
Blueberries . . . . 1½ to 3	Beets . . . . 2 to 3½
Cherries. . . . . . . 2 to 2½	Cauliflower 3
Grapes 4	Corn. . . . . 3 to 6
Peaches . . . . 2 to 3	Peas. . . . . 3 to 6
Pears . . . . 2 to 3	Peppers. 3
Raspberries . . . . 1½ to 3	Spinach. . . . . 2 to 3
Strawberries. . . . 1½ to 3	Tomatoes . . . . 2½ to 3½

September

6   *Monday*

Labor Day
Last Quarter Moon

**The hardest work of all
is to do nothing.**

–American proverb

7   *Tuesday*

Seed new lawns
before the leaves fall.

8   *Wednesday*

One Brazil nut a
day gives you the
selenium (an
antioxidant mineral)
you need.

9   *Thursday*

Admission Day (Calif.)

For the sweetest cider,
do not use apples that
are rotten ripe, and
don't press them
during a heavy rain.

SEPTEMBER • 2004   OCTOBER • 2004

S	M	T	W	T	F	S
			1	2	3	4
5	6	7	8	9	10	11
12	13	14	15	16	17	18
19	20	21	22	23	24	25
26	27	28	29	30		

S	M	T	W	T	F	S
					1	2
3	4	5	6	7	8	9
10	11	12	13	14	15	16
17	18	19	20	21	22	23
24	25	26	27	28	29	30
31						

Friday 10

Frequent hand washing (five times per day) can cut colds by almost half.

Peace is the fairest form of happiness.
–William Ellery Channing, American clergyman (1780–1842)

Saturday 11

Grandparents Day

Sunday 12

It takes a long time to become young.
–Pablo Picasso, Spanish painter (1881–1973)

REMINDERS

September

13 *Monday*

If a crab-apple tree hangs over the well and blooms out of season, there will be marriage and fertility.

14 *Tuesday*

New Moon

The 2005 Old Farmer's Almanac goes on sale today.

15 *Wednesday*

Try a dab of honey to heal cold sores or canker sores.

16 *Thursday*

Rosh Hashanah

Good things require time.

SEPTEMBER • 2004   OCTOBER • 2004

S	M	T	W	T	F	S
			1	2	3	4
5	6	7	8	9	10	11
12	13	14	15	16	17	18
19	20	21	22	23	24	25
26	27	28	29	30		

S	M	T	W	T	F	S
					1	2
3	4	5	6	7	8	9
10	11	12	13	14	15	16
17	18	19	20	21	22	23
24	25	26	27	28	29	30
31						

Citizenship Day

Friday

17

*September and October
are the months for
planting peony roots.*
–Katharine S. White,
American editor (1892–1977)

Make extra waffles
and freeze them for
another day.

Saturday

18

Married in September's
golden glow,
Smooth and serene your
life will go.

Sunday

19

REMINDERS

September

20 *Monday*

I ain't in no slump. I just ain't hittin'.
–Yogi Berra, professional baseball player (b. 1925)

21 *Tuesday*

St. Matthew's Day
First Quarter Moon

St. Matthee,
Shut up the bee.

22 *Wednesday*

Autumnal Equinox

For mulch, use a string trimmer to shred leaves in a plastic garbage can. (Wear goggles!)

23 *Thursday*

Libra's balanced Scales
(Sept. 23 to Oct. 22)
say, "I weigh."

SEPTEMBER • 2004   OCTOBER • 2004

S	M	T	W	T	F	S
			1	2	3	4
5	6	7	8	9	10	11
12	13	14	15	16	17	18
19	20	21	22	23	24	25
26	27	28	29	30		

S	M	T	W	T	F	S
					1	2
3	4	5	6	7	8	9
10	11	12	13	14	15	16
17	18	19	20	21	22	23
24	25	26	27	28	29	30
31						

Friday 24

If you like 'McIntosh' apples, try fuller-flavored 'Macoun'—a 'McIntosh' crossed with 'Jersey Black'.

Saturday 25

Yom Kippur

I've learned that it's taking me a long time to become the person I want to be.
–Anonymous

Sunday 26

Tuck a sprig of dried lavender or other fragrant herb inside sofa-pillow covers.

REMINDERS

SEPTEMBER

27 *Monday*

Prune grapevines, and water shrubs before the ground freezes.

28 *Tuesday*

Full Harvest Moon

Onion skins very thin,
Mild winter coming in.

29 *Wednesday*

Michaelmas Day

Goose was the traditional fare on the feast day of St. Michael.

30 *Thursday*

For hoarseness, swallow slowly the juice of radishes.
—18th-century remedy

It's time to order your 2005 Engagement Calendar

■ The 2005 Old Farmer's Almanac Engagement Calendar is ready now. Order it today and have it available to start jotting down important appointments and events.

ENGAGEMENT CALENDAR • ITEM: OF05CEG $14.95 each

Would you like to receive this calendar PLUS a free gift each year AND save the bother of reordering?

Join thousands of like-minded folks in our Engagement Calendar Continuity Program and receive this calendar PLUS a free copy of The Old Farmer's Almanac automatically each year.

Here's how the Continuity Program works: We will mail a reminder in July and provide you with a postage-paid reply card to notify us of any changes, or to tell us to cancel the shipment. You will always have 30 days to respond. If you wish to receive the next year's calendar, you do not have to do a thing. We'll ship it (and your FREE Almanac) automatically in early September. You may cancel this program at any time. **ENGAGEMENT CALENDAR WITH CONTINUITY PROGRAM ENROLLMENT AND FREE ALMANAC • ITEM: OF05CEGC** $14.95

MORE PRODUCTS AVAILABLE—Information on reverse side. ORDER TODAY!

4 ORDERING OPTIONS

- **Mail this form with payment:** The Old Farmer's Almanac, P.O. Box 37370, Boone, IA 50037-0370
- **Phone: 800-223-3166** for credit card orders 7 A.M.–11 P.M. Mon.–Fri., and 8 A.M.–6 P.M. Sat.–Sun. (CST)
- **Fax:** 515-433-5001
- **On-line:** www.almanac.com/go/ecr2005

SOLD TO:

Name

Mailing address

City   State   Zip

Daytime telephone*

E-mail address*

SHIP TO (if different from "SOLD TO" address):

Name

Mailing address

City   State   Zip

Daytime telephone*

E-mail address*

* Telephone and e-mail information is helpful to us if we need to contact you about your order. We do not share our customer information with anyone.

ITEM	DESCRIPTION	QUANTITY	EACH	TOTAL
OF05CEG	2005 Engagement Calendar only		$14.95	
OF05CEGC	2005 Engagement Calendar with FREE *Old Farmer's Almanac* and Continuity Program enrollment		$14.95	
OF05CFC	2005 Country Calendar (wall)		$9.99	
OF05CGC	2005 Gardening Calendar (wall)		$ 7.99	
OF05CHC	2005 Herbs Calendar (wall)		$ 9.99	
OF05CWW	2005 Weather Watcher's Calendar (wall)		$ 7.99	
		SUBTOTAL	$	
		Add shipping and handling	$	4.95
		TOTAL AMOUNT	$	

Key: **CAFECROE**

PAYMENT TERMS:

☐ Personal check or money order in U.S. dollars drawn on a U.S. bank is enclosed.

Charge my   ☐ Visa   ☐ MasterCard   ☐ American Express   ☐ Discover/NOVUS

Account number   Expiration date

Signature (required for credit card orders)

Visit our Web site often to see what's new! www.almanac.com/go/ecr2005a

Other fine products from The Old Farmer's Almanac

NEW FOR 2005!

The 2005 Old Farmer's Almanac Country Calendar

■ Introducing our newest wall calendar! You'll be proud to display this exquisite calendar wherever you call home. It features beautiful color photographs plus the best days for fishing, planting, and setting eggs; observations from the Old Farmer about farm life; proverbs; Moon phases; holiday celebrations; and more. 10⅞" x 21¾" open. **COUNTRY CALENDAR • ITEM: OF05CFC** $9.99 each

The 2005 Old Farmer's Almanac Gardening Calendar

■ Now in its 28th year! Calendars may come and go, but The Old Farmer's Almanac Gardening Calendar is a classic that endures. Beautifully illustrated in full color. Useful tips for every gardener, from novice to backyard naturalist. Includes outdoor planting guide for the United States and Canada. 10⅞" x 16¾" open. **GARDENING CALENDAR • ITEM: OF05CGC** $7.99 each

The 2005 Old Farmer's Almanac Herbs Calendar

■ Gardening, cooking, and healing with herbs. If you are interested in herbs on any level, you'll love this calendar. Illustrated with handsome botanical artistry, each month features one herb, with history, gardening tips, a recipe, and other ways to use it around the home. 10⅞" x 21¾" open. **HERBS CALENDAR • ITEM: OF05CHC** $9.99 each

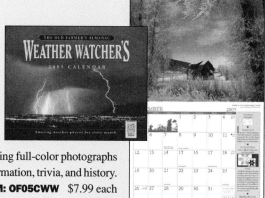

The 2005 Old Farmer's Almanac Weather Watcher's Calendar

■ Good or bad, the weather is a fascinating subject. Here's the ultimate calendar for your favorite weather watcher. Amazing full-color photographs of unusual weather phenomena. Monthly weather-related information, trivia, and history. 10⅞" x 16¾" open. **WEATHER WATCHER'S CALENDAR • ITEM: OF05CWW** $7.99 each

---

To see all our Old Farmer's Almanac products, visit our On-line Store:

www.almanac.com/go/ecr2005a

OCTOBER

Evening gray and morning red Will pour down rain on the traveler's head.

Friday

1

Feeling blue? Listen to music and avoid heavy foods.

Saturday

2

Leaf peeper's color guide: White ash and witch hazel typically show purple leaves.

Sunday

3

REMINDERS

OCTOBER

with *The Old Farmer's Almanac*

125 Years Ago

The corn is to be got in, the potatoes to be dug, the apples to be picked, and a thousand things to be done to get ready for winter. But the days are cool, and there is no time of the year when we feel so much like work. Winter grain may still be sown, and fall ploughing is still in order. Both oxen and horses can work better now than at any other time; and so it costs less than it will in the spring, to say nothing of the saving of time. It is the best time, too, to hurry up the fattening of all kinds of stock. Animals take on fat faster now than in cold weather, while the flies trouble them less than they did a month or two ago. The roots keep on growing; but if there are any weeds, don't fail to pull them to stop them from going to seed. The growth of the year in forest and fruit trees is about finished, and so it is a good time to cut timber. It will last longer and dry better cut now than at any other time. Loam and muck may be hauled into the yard to use as a compost. It is rather late to sow grass-seed and winter grains, and if we failed to get it in last month, better wait till the end of next, and sow it just before the ground freezes. It is better to sow then than to wait till spring.

—*The Old Farmer's Almanac*

FULL-MOON LORE

The Full Hunter's Moon occurs on October 27 in 2004. The leaves are falling and the game is fattened—now is the time for hunting and laying in a store of provisions for the long winter ahead. October's Moon is also known as the Travel Moon.

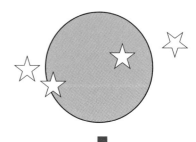

Light or white frosts are always followed by wet weather, either the same day or three days after.

Secrets of the Zodiac

LIBRA

SEPTEMBER 23–OCTOBER 22

You are the tactful diplomats of the zodiac. Ever concerned with the impact of your words and actions, you strive for harmony in all things. You weigh and balance with careful deliberation and thoroughly think through all your plans and activities. Good at seeing all sides of a situation, you are often drawn to fields dealing with the law or courts. Justice is your companion.

Although balance is your watchword, you do not maintain center at all times; rather, you continuously swing and sway back and forth, always striving for the central point. If you work too many hours one week, you will sleep in a lot during the next. You intuitively sense where to fulfill your needs.

Your sense of color and design is usually very high, and you possess a highly developed aesthetic sense. Because of this, many of you enjoy careers having to do with beauty: art, interior decorating, modeling, or design. You also do well in partnerships due to your need to relate, but you should guard against giving away your power for fear of loneliness.

JUNCO CORN BREAD

Here's a hearty cold-weather treat that juncos will love!

- 3 cups cornmeal
- 2 teaspoons baking powder
- ½ cup fat (meat drippings or lard)
- 3 cups water

■ Mix all the ingredients together, and bake in a deep pan at 375°F for 30 to 35 minutes. Reduce heat if bread looks as if it is forming a hard crust. May be doubled or halved. Place into mesh bags and hang outdoors.

FOOD FOR THE BIRD FEEDER

Bird	Millet (white proso)	Niger (thistle seeds)	Oranges and grapefruit	Peanuts	Safflower seeds	Suet	Sunflower seeds
Blue jay				✓	✓		✓
Bunting	✓	✓			✓		✓
Cardinal	✓			✓	✓		✓
Cedar waxwing			✓				
Chickadee	✓			✓	✓	✓	✓
Crossbill	✓				✓		✓
Finch	✓	✓	✓		✓		✓
Grosbeak	✓			✓	✓		✓
Junco	✓	✓					✓
Mourning dove	✓				✓		✓
Nuthatch	✓			✓	✓	✓	✓
Oriole			✓				
Pine siskin	✓	✓	✓		✓		✓
Sparrow	✓				✓		✓
Tanager			✓				
Titmouse	✓			✓	✓	✓	✓
Woodpecker				✓		✓	

October

---

4 *Monday*

A child is fed with milk and praise.

–Mary Ann Lamb, English
poet (1764–1847)

---

5 *Tuesday*

To preserve fall
leaves, boil 1 part
glycerine with 2 parts
water. Soak leaf stems
overnight in the
solution.

---

6 *Wednesday*

Last Quarter Moon

Store pickles and
canned goods away
from direct sunlight
or heat.

---

7 *Thursday*

Water evergreen
hollies well before the
ground freezes.

OCTOBER • 2004   NOVEMBER • 2004

S M T W T F S   S M T W T F S
            1 2   1 2 3 4 5 6
3 4 5 6 7 8 9   7 8 9 10 11 12 13
10 11 12 13 14 15 16   14 15 16 17 18 19 20
17 18 19 20 21 22 23   21 22 23 24 25 26 27
24 25 26 27 28 29 30   28 29 30
31

Friday

8

Don't judge a 'Golden Russet' apple by its skin; it's full of flavor!

Saturday

9

Leif Eriksson Day

When deer are in a gray coat in October, expect a hard winter.

Sunday

10

Leaf peeper's color guide: Scarlet oak, sumac, and tupelo show red leaves.

REMINDERS

OCTOBER

11	*Monday*	Columbus Day (observed) Thanksgiving (Canada)

Better some of a pudding than none of a pie.

12	*Tuesday*	Buy pumpkins with stems attached— they'll keep better.

13	*Wednesday*	New Moon

Weather-strip doors and windows for winter.

14	*Thursday*	*For age and want, save while you may; No morning sun lasts a whole day.*

–Benjamin Franklin, American statesman (1706–1790)

OCTOBER • 2004   NOVEMBER • 2004

S M T W T F S   S M T W T F S
          1 2   1 2 3 4 5 6
3 4 5 6 7 8 9   7 8 9 10 11 12 13
10 11 12 13 14 15 16   14 15 16 17 18 19 20
17 18 19 20 21 22 23   21 22 23 24 25 26 27
24 25 26 27 28 29 30   28 29 30
31

First day of Ramadan   *Friday* **15**

*Hunger increases the
understanding.*
–Lithuanian proverb

**The fourth day of the
new Moon is propitious for
starting construction.**

Saturday **16**

**Married when leaves
in October thin,
Toil and hardship for
you gain.**

Sunday **17**

REMINDERS

OCTOBER

18 *Monday*

Look for warm, dry weather on this day of "Saint Luke's Little Summer."

19 *Tuesday*

Leaf peeper's color guide: Beech, birch, butternut, and elm show yellow leaves.

20 *Wednesday*

First Quarter Moon

Inspect woodstove pipes for creosote buildup.

21 *Thursday*

Watch for Orionid meteors at predawn.

OCTOBER • 2004   NOVEMBER • 2004

S	M	T	W	T	F	S
					1	2
3	4	5	6	7	8	9
10	11	12	13	14	15	16
17	18	19	20	21	22	23
24	25	26	27	28	29	30
31						

S	M	T	W	T	F	S
	1	2	3	4	5	6
7	8	9	10	11	12	13
14	15	16	17	18	19	20
21	22	23	24	25	26	27
28	29	30				

Friday 22

Dip candle ends into very hot water, then fit them into holders while the wax is soft.

Saturday 23

Scorpio's Scorpion (Oct. 23 to Nov. 22) may be possessive and says, "I control."

Sunday 24

United Nations Day

By wisdom peace, by peace plenty.

REMINDERS

OCTOBER

25 *Monday*

> There are tones of
> voice that mean more
> than words.
>
> –Robert Frost, American poet
> (1874–1963)

26 *Tuesday*

Toasting increases
the flavor of sesame,
mustard, and cumin
seeds.

27 *Wednesday*

Full Hunter's Moon

Native Americans
ate raw onions to cure
insomnia.

28 *Thursday*

Halloween idea:
Become a
1950s carhop with
roller skates, an apron,
and a tray.

OCTOBER • 2004   NOVEMBER • 2004

S	M	T	W	T	F	S
					1	2
3	4	5	6	7	8	9
10	11	12	13	14	15	16
17	18	19	20	21	22	23
24	25	26	27	28	29	30
31						

S	M	T	W	T	F	S
	1	2	3	4	5	6
7	8	9	10	11	12	13
14	15	16	17	18	19	20
21	22	23	24	25	26	27
28	29	30				

Friday **29**

I too have a new plaything, the best I ever had—a wood-lot.

–Ralph Waldo Emerson,
American writer (1803–1882)

Saturday **30**

Pumpkin seeds may help ease benign prostate problems.

Sunday **31**

Halloween
Daylight Saving Time ends
at 2:00 A.M.

When you reset your clocks (twice a year), also check your smoke-alarm batteries.

REMINDERS

NOVEMBER

with *The Old Farmer's Almanac*

125 Years Ago

FARMER'S CALENDAR, NOVEMBER 1879

The roots must come in now, and the harvest will soon end. The frost will close the ground all at once, and it will not do to be caught napping. Mangolds, you know, are a little tender, but the swedes will stand it to the last, though there is not much time to lose with them. All kinds of stock are fond of roots, and they make a change, at any rate, from dry hay through the long cold months. But the pumpkins are good yet, and the cows like a few every day. They are a great help now while they are changing from pasture to winter feed. Follow them with the round turnip, then with the swede, and last of all, the mangolds. Grape-vines and fruit-trees can be trimmed now. Why not try a few more small fruits? They can be set out now, but it is about as well to wait till spring. Don't feed the lots too close. It is a bad plan to let the cattle gnaw them down to the ground; kills the grass, you know, and runs out the land. It's best to house the cattle. It will do them no good to lie out-doors these cold frosty nights. Warm shelter is the secret of success with all kinds of stock. Snug up things, and get ready for a downright jolly Thanksgiving.

–The Old Farmer's Almanac

FULL-MOON LORE

The Full Beaver Moon occurs on November 26 in 2004. It is a sign of freezing weather to come. For Algonquin tribes, this Moon was a time to set beaver traps before the swamps froze to ensure a supply of warm winter furs. November's Moon is also known as the Frost Moon.

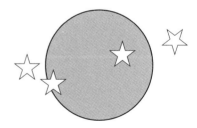

Ice in November

brings mud in

December.

Secrets of the Zodiac

SCORPIO

OCTOBER 23–NOVEMBER 22

You are the strongest members of the zodiac. Because of this, there is no middle road for you: Choose the high road or the low road, but choose you must. Unlike the other astrological signs of strength, you don't waste it showing it off. You wait until you truly want something and then focus your will on your goals. You have the capacity to get what you want.

You understand the intricacies and the innuendos of power. Using advantage, you always have a plan, and you build upon your plans to help improve the future. Intuitively, you sense ulterior motives and hidden agendas, and your shrewdness amazes and intrigues others.

Because of your strength, you often intimidate other people. As long as your own motivations remain pure, you needn't worry. Choosing the low road, however, will always get you in the end. Spread your wings of protection over your brood and fly like the eagle, and there will be no stopping you.

EASY SCRUB

¾ cup baking soda
¼ cup borax
dishwashing liquid

■ Combine the baking soda and borax. Mix in enough dishwashing liquid to make a smooth paste. If you prefer a pleasant smell, add ¼ teaspoon lemon juice to the paste. Use on kitchen counters and similar surfaces.

TABLE OF MEASURES

Liquid Measure
3 teaspoons = 1 tablespoon
2 tablespoons = ⅛ cup or 1 ounce
4 tablespoons = ¼ cup or 2 ounces
6 tablespoons = ⅜ cup or 3 ounces
7 tablespoons = ⅓ cup
8 tablespoons = ½ cup or 4 ounces
16 tablespoons = 1 cup
1 cup = ½ pint or 8 ounces
2 cups = 1 pint or 16 ounces
4 cups = 1 quart
2 pints = 1 quart
4 quarts = 1 gallon

Dry Measure
2 pints = 1 quart
4 quarts = 1 gallon
2 gallons = 1 peck
4 pecks = 1 bushel

Metric Liquid Measure
1 cup = .24 liter
1 pint = .47 liter
1 quart = .95 liter
1 gallon = 3.79 liters
1 deciliter = .21 pints
1 liter = 1.057 quarts

Metric Dry Measure
1 ounce = 28 grams
1 pound = 454 grams
1 gram = .035 ounce
1 kilogram = 2.2 pounds

November

1 *Monday*

Set trees at Allhallontide (first week in November), and command them to prosper.

2 *Tuesday*   Election Day

A great nose indicates a great man—
Genial, courteous,
intellectual,
Virile, courageous.
–Edmond Rostand, French playwright (1868–1918)

3 *Wednesday*

For an "old cough," Native Americans recommended blueberry juice or blueberry syrup.

4 *Thursday*   Will Rogers Day (Okla.)

Everybody is ignorant, only on different subjects.
–Will Rogers, American actor (1879–1935)

NOVEMBER • 2004   DECEMBER • 2004

S	M	T	W	T	F	S		S	M	T	W	T	F	S
	1	2	3	4	5	6					1	2	3	4
7	8	9	10	11	12	13		5	6	7	8	9	10	11
14	15	16	17	18	19	20		12	13	14	15	16	17	18
21	22	23	24	25	26	27		19	20	21	22	23	24	25
28	29	30						26	27	28	29	30	31	

Last Quarter Moon

Friday

5

Plant tulip bulbs
twice as deep as their
height.

Protect fruit trees
from mice with a tree
wrap at the base.
Remove in spring.

Saturday

6

To bring good luck,
collect your eggs by daylight,
never after nightfall.

Sunday

7

REMINDERS

November

8 *Monday*

A capful of baby oil added to mop water will help preserve linoleum floors.

9 *Tuesday*

Man is a dog's idea of what God should be.
—Holbrook Jackson, English journalist (1874–1948)

10 *Wednesday*

Keep spider plants, chrysanthemums, or golden pothos on your desk to reduce indoor pollutants.

11 *Thursday*

Veterans Day
Remembrance Day (Canada)

We must always have old memories and young hopes.
—Arsène Houssaye, French writer (1815–1896)

NOVEMBER • 2004   DECEMBER • 2004

S M T W T F S   S M T W T F S
         1 2 3 4 5 6   1 2 3 4
7 8 9 10 11 12 13   5 6 7 8 9 10 11
14 15 16 17 18 19 20   12 13 14 15 16 17 18
21 22 23 24 25 26 27   19 20 21 22 23 24 25
28 29 30   26 27 28 29 30 31

New Moon

Friday 12

Indian summer occurs anytime between St. Martin's Day (November 11) and November 20.

Mint teas generally relieve indigestion, but peppermint may aggravate heartburn.

Saturday 13

Remove summer screens now to let in sunshine and reduce your heating bill.

Sunday 14

REMINDERS

Complement this calendar with daily weather and Almanac wit and wisdom at www.almanac.com.

November

15 *Monday*

Nothing hinders a cure so much as frequent change of medicine.
—Lucius Annaeus Seneca, Roman statesman (c. 4 B.C.–A.D. 65)

16 *Tuesday*

Want to learn a new skill? Volunteer at a place that can teach it.

17 *Wednesday*

Fertilize shade trees now.

18 *Thursday*

The thing you have to be prepared for is that other people don't always dream your dream.
—Linda Ronstadt, American singer (b. 1946)

November • 2004   December • 2004

S M T W T F S   S M T W T F S
      1 2 3 4 5 6   1 2 3 4
7 8 9 10 11 12 13   5 6 7 8 9 10 11
14 15 16 17 18 19 20   12 13 14 15 16 17 18
21 22 23 24 25 26 27   19 20 21 22 23 24 25
28 29 30   26 27 28 29 30 31

Discovery Day (Puerto Rico)
First Quarter Moon

Friday 19

Clean or replace
furnace air filters.

Saturday 20

Married in veils of
November mist,
Fortune your wedding ring
has kissed.

Sunday 21

Begin making
pomanders and winter
potpourri now.

REMINDERS

Complement this calendar with daily weather and Almanac wit and wisdom at www.almanac.com.

November

22 *Monday*

When poaching fish, the water should "tremble," not boil.

23 *Tuesday*

Sagittarius's Archer (Nov. 23 to Dec. 21) is a high-minded ethicist, with the motto "I philosophize."

24 *Wednesday*

Man is the only animal that blushes. Or needs to.
–Mark Twain, American writer (1835–1910)

25 *Thursday*

Thanksgiving

Add a little stuffing to pan juices for thicker, tastier gravy.

NOVEMBER • 2004

S	M	T	W	T	F	S
	1	2	3	4	5	6
7	8	9	10	11	12	13
14	15	16	17	18	19	20
21	22	23	24	25	26	27
28	29	30				

DECEMBER • 2004

S	M	T	W	T	F	S
			1	2	3	4
5	6	7	8	9	10	11
12	13	14	15	16	17	18
19	20	21	22	23	24	25
26	27	28	29	30	31	

Acadian Day (La.)
Full Beaver Moon

Friday 26

For wet cleaning jobs up high, wear a wristband to stop drips from running down your arm.

Making fruitcake? Freeze citrons for easier chopping. Dip knife into hot water.

Saturday 27

John F. Kennedy Day (Mass.)

Sunday 28

Mankind must put an end to war or war will put an end to mankind.
–John F. Kennedy, 35th U.S. president (1917–1963)

REMINDERS

29 *Monday*

Well-lit rooms help combat seasonal affective disorder (SAD).

30 *Tuesday*

The future ain't what it used to be.

–Yogi Berra, professional baseball player (b. 1925)

1 *Wednesday*

Gradual exercise repairs weak muscles that account for 80 percent of backaches.

2 *Thursday*

Hang mistletoe in the kitchen; remove a berry (poisonous!) for each kiss redeemed.

NOVEMBER • 2004

DECEMBER • 2004

S M T W T F S
1 2 3 4 5 6
7 8 9 10 11 12 13
14 15 16 17 18 19 20
21 22 23 24 25 26 27
28 29 30

S M T W T F S
1 2 3 4
5 6 7 8 9 10 11
12 13 14 15 16 17 18
19 20 21 22 23 24 25
26 27 28 29 30 31

Assemble special
recipes in a gift book
for newlyweds and
college students.

Friday

3

Last Quarter Moon

☆ ☆

Saturday

4

Shovel snow with
knees bent, back
straight, and head up.
Lift with legs and arms.

Start paper-white
narcissus bulbs now
for indoor blooms at
Christmas.

Sunday

5

REMINDERS

DECEMBER

with The Old Farmer's Almanac

125 Years Ago

If the ground is not covered with snow, it is best to haul out manure and spread it as a top-dressing on grass-land. Some fields are so soft that they are poached and cut up at other seasons; but they are hard enough now, and a good dressing will help them and keep up the growth of grass. It is a good rule to spread right from the cart, far better than to dump in heaps to lie over winter. Fields that were fed down closely in the fall need this protection very much, and the manure cannot be put to better use. It will not do to rob our grass-lands to feed the hoed crops. That has been the fault of too much of our farming, and it is time to change it and try something else. Grass or hay is the basis of all our prosperity, and this is a fact that we cannot wink out of sight. The care of stock will take up a good deal of time now, and we must not forget that warm shelter is as necessary for animals as it is for us. I like to feed some meal with the coarse hay and cornstalks, and the fine-ground meal is by far the best. In fact, it does not pay to feed coarseground grains of any kind; the loss is too great. It is a good plan to settle up accounts and begin the new year all square.

—The Old Farmer's Almanac

FULL-MOON LORE

The Full Cold Moon occurs on December 26 in 2004. Also called the Long Nights Moon among some Native American tribes, this is when the winter cold fastens its grip and the nights become long and dark.

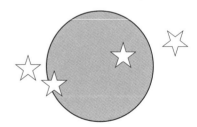

Many stars

in winter

indicate frost.

Secrets of the Zodiac

SAGITTARIUS

NOVEMBER 23–DECEMBER 21

You are the philosophers of the zodiac. On a personal mission to discover Truth (with a capital "T"), you intuitively understand that there is more to life and living than what is apparent on the surface. You seek to know the inner causes of the outer manifestations, and yours is a spiritual quest.

Loving both the country and the city, your ideal would be to own two homes. You feel drawn to the wide expanses, but the hustle and bustle of town also excites you. Interested in just about everything, you are a wonderful conversationalist—so much so that you are often bored when speaking with signs other than your own. Your need for freedom is very strong, and you quickly tire of jobs that keep you stationary.

As you quite literally need to move about, you can often be found in groups traveling to foreign countries and faraway places. Generally athletic, you enjoy safaris into the outback and hikes up the mountains. If you can't travel physically, you will travel intellectually, and your nose can often be found in a book.

CANINE COOKIES

Give dogs a special treat this holiday season.

3 ½ cups whole-wheat flour
3 cups rolled oats
½ cup powdered milk
½ cup bacon grease
2 teaspoons cod-liver oil
2 eggs
1 ½ cups instant beef or chicken bouillon,
*   or chicken stock*

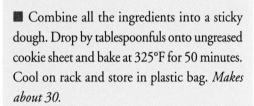

■ Combine all the ingredients into a sticky dough. Drop by tablespoonfuls onto ungreased cookie sheet and bake at 325°F for 50 minutes. Cool on rack and store in plastic bag. *Makes about 30.*

HOUSEPLANT HARMONIES

■ Experiments conducted in a controlled environment during the 1960s and 1970s suggest that you may want to consider the health and well-being of your houseplants when making musical selections.

TYPE OF MUSIC	EFFECT ON PLANT GROWTH
Classical	Lush and abundant growth; good root development
Indian devotional	Lush and abundant growth; good root development
Jazz	Abundant growth
Country	No abnormal growth reaction
Silence	No abnormal growth reaction
Rock 'n' roll	Poor growth; roots scrawny and sparse
White noise	Plants died quickly

December

6 · Monday

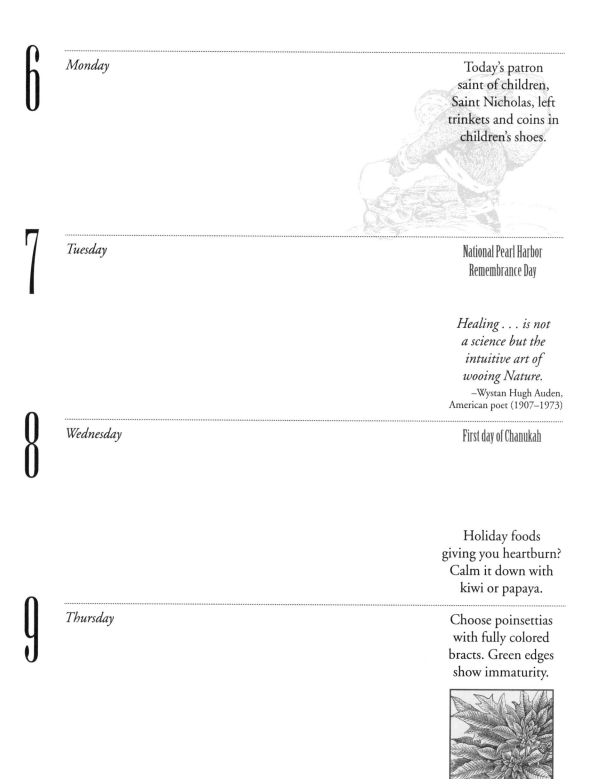

Today's patron saint of children, Saint Nicholas, left trinkets and coins in children's shoes.

7 · Tuesday

National Pearl Harbor Remembrance Day

Healing . . . is not a science but the intuitive art of wooing Nature.
—Wystan Hugh Auden, American poet (1907–1973)

8 · Wednesday

First day of Chanukah

Holiday foods giving you heartburn? Calm it down with kiwi or papaya.

9 · Thursday

Choose poinsettias with fully colored bracts. Green edges show immaturity.

DECEMBER • 2004   JANUARY • 2005

S	M	T	W	T	F	S
			1	2	3	4
5	6	7	8	9	10	11
12	13	14	15	16	17	18
19	20	21	22	23	24	25
26	27	28	29	30	31	

S	M	T	W	T	F	S
						1
2	3	4	5	6	7	8
9	10	11	12	13	14	15
16	17	18	19	20	21	22
23	24	25	26	27	28	29
30	31					

Small gifts make friends, great ones make enemies.

Friday 10

New Moon

Saturday 11

Make entertaining simple—host a potluck dinner.

For good luck, stir the Christmas pudding from east to west, or "sun-wise."

Sunday 12

REMINDERS

DECEMBER

13 *Monday*

Use essential oils of clary sage or cinnamon as room fresheners; they fight bacteria.

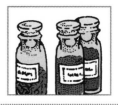

14 *Tuesday*

Abstain from all eccentricities. Take a medium between nature and fashion.

–Ladies Indispensable Assistant, 1852

15 *Wednesday*

Bill of Rights Day

For insomnia, drink warm milk with chopped garlic simmered in it.

16 *Thursday*

In lore, Halcyon Days promise 14 days of calm waters around the winter solstice for nesting kingfishers.

DECEMBER • 2004   JANUARY • 2005

S	M	T	W	T	F	S
			1	2	3	4
5	6	7	8	9	10	11
12	13	14	15	16	17	18
19	20	21	22	23	24	25
26	27	28	29	30	31	

S	M	T	W	T	F	S
						1
2	3	4	5	6	7	8
9	10	11	12	13	14	15
16	17	18	19	20	21	22
23	24	25	26	27	28	29
30	31					

Wright Brothers Day

Friday

17

Light a candle for
the Roman Saturnalia
(Dec. 17 to 23),
a time of peace and
feasting.

First Quarter Moon

Saturday

18

Mist houseplants
frequently during the
dry winter months.

Sunday

19

Married in days
of December cheer,
Love's star shines brighter
from year to year.

REMINDERS

December

20 *Monday*

Sprinkle baking soda on carpets to deodorize; leave on for an hour, then vacuum.

21 *Tuesday*

Winter Solstice

Beautiful Soup, so rich and green, Waiting in a hot tureen!
—Lewis Carroll, English writer (1832–1898)

22 *Wednesday*

Practical Capricorn the Goat (Dec. 22 to Jan. 19) says, "I master."

23 *Thursday*

Replace toothbrushes regularly, or soak them in mouthwash, to discourage colds.

DECEMBER • 2004

S	M	T	W	T	F	S
			1	2	3	4
5	6	7	8	9	10	11
12	13	14	15	16	17	18
19	20	21	22	23	24	25
26	27	28	29	30	31	

JANUARY • 2005

S	M	T	W	T	F	S
						1
2	3	4	5	6	7	8
9	10	11	12	13	14	15
16	17	18	19	20	21	22
23	24	25	26	27	28	29
30	31					

Friday

24

A good time to read
O. Henry's short story
The Gift of the Magi.

Saturday

25

𝕮𝖍𝖗𝖎𝖘𝖙𝖒𝖆𝖘 𝕯𝖆𝖞

At Christmas meadows
green,
at Easter covered
with frost.

Sunday

26

Boxing Day (Canada)
Full Cold Moon

Today is the first day
of Kwanzaa. *Kwanza*
is Kiswahili for "first."

REMINDERS

December ❧ January 2005

27 *Monday*

Those who have lain up dry wood will not wear out bellows.
–The [Old] Farmer's Almanac, 1801

28 *Tuesday*

Even the ancient Romans knew that exercise, massages, and baths helped cure winter doldrums.

29 *Wednesday*

Shipshape is upright! Keep buckets and open vessels right side up, or risk bad luck.

30 *Thursday*

Clear your mind of can't.
–Dr. Samuel Johnson, English writer (1709–1784)

DECEMBER • 2004

S	M	T	W	T	F	S
			1	2	3	4
5	6	7	8	9	10	11
12	13	14	15	16	17	18
19	20	21	22	23	24	25
26	27	28	29	30	31	

JANUARY • 2005

S	M	T	W	T	F	S
						1
2	3	4	5	6	7	8
9	10	11	12	13	14	15
16	17	18	19	20	21	22
23	24	25	26	27	28	29
30	31					

Friday

31

**Dream of birds and you
dream of friends and fortune.**

New Year's Day

Saturday

1

**A good beginning makes
a good ending.**

*Peace . . . can only
be achieved by
understanding.*
–Albert Einstein, American
physicist (1879–1955)

Sunday

2

REMINDERS

2005

JANUARY

S	M	T	W	T	F	S
						1
2	3	4	5	6	7	8
9	10	11	12	13	14	15
16	17	18	19	20	21	22
23	24	25	26	27	28	29
30	31					

FEBRUARY

S	M	T	W	T	F	S
		1	2	3	4	5
6	7	8	9	10	11	12
13	14	15	16	17	18	19
20	21	22	23	24	25	26
27	28					

MARCH

S	M	T	W	T	F	S
		1	2	3	4	5
6	7	8	9	10	11	12
13	14	15	16	17	18	19
20	21	22	23	24	25	26
27	28	29	30	31		

ADVANCE PLANNER

_____

_____

_____

_____

_____

_____

APRIL

S	M	T	W	T	F	S
					1	2
3	4	5	6	7	8	9
10	11	12	13	14	15	16
17	18	19	20	21	22	23
24	25	26	27	28	29	30

MAY

S	M	T	W	T	F	S
1	2	3	4	5	6	7
8	9	10	11	12	13	14
15	16	17	18	19	20	21
22	23	24	25	26	27	28
29	30	31				

JUNE

S	M	T	W	T	F	S
			1	2	3	4
5	6	7	8	9	10	11
12	13	14	15	16	17	18
19	20	21	22	23	24	25
26	27	28	29	30		

ADVANCE PLANNER

_____

_____

_____

_____

_____

_____

July

S	M	T	W	T	F	S
					1	2
3	4	5	6	7	8	9
10	11	12	13	14	15	16
17	18	19	20	21	22	23
24	25	26	27	28	29	30
31						

August

S	M	T	W	T	F	S
	1	2	3	4	5	6
7	8	9	10	11	12	13
14	15	16	17	18	19	20
21	22	23	24	25	26	27
28	29	30	31			

September

S	M	T	W	T	F	S
				1	2	3
4	5	6	7	8	9	10
11	12	13	14	15	16	17
18	19	20	21	22	23	24
25	26	27	28	29	30	

ADVANCE PLANNER

_____

_____

_____

_____

_____

_____

October

S	M	T	W	T	F	S
						1
2	3	4	5	6	7	8
9	10	11	12	13	14	15
16	17	18	19	20	21	22
23	24	25	26	27	28	29
30	31					

November

S	M	T	W	T	F	S
		1	2	3	4	5
6	7	8	9	10	11	12
13	14	15	16	17	18	19
20	21	22	23	24	25	26
27	28	29	30			

December

S	M	T	W	T	F	S
				1	2	3
4	5	6	7	8	9	10
11	12	13	14	15	16	17
18	19	20	21	22	23	24
25	26	27	28	29	30	31

ADVANCE PLANNER

_____

_____

_____

_____

_____

_____

Addresses and Phone Numbers

Name	Home
Address	Office
	Cell
E-mail	Fax
Web	

Name	Home
Address	Office
	Cell
E-mail	Fax
Web	

Name	Home
Address	Office
	Cell
E-mail	Fax
Web	

Name	Home
Address	Office
	Cell
E-mail	Fax
Web	

Name	Home
Address	Office
	Cell
E-mail	Fax
Web	

Name	Home
Address	Office
	Cell
E-mail	Fax
Web	

Name	Home
Address	Office
	Cell
E-mail	Fax
Web	

Name	Home
Address	Office
	Cell
E-mail	Fax
Web	

Name	Home
Address	Office
	Cell
E-mail	Fax
Web	

Name	Home
Address	Office
	Cell
E-mail	Fax
Web	

Name	Home
Address	Office
	Cell
E-mail	Fax
Web	

Name	Home
Address	Office
	Cell
E-mail	Fax
Web	

Name	Home
Address	Office
	Cell
E-mail	Fax
Web	

Name	Home
Address	Office
	Cell
E-mail	Fax
Web	

BIRTHDAYS AND ANNIVERSARIES

Name	Birthday	Anniversary